This edition first published in 1993 by
Sunburst Books, Deacon House, 65 Old Church Street,
London, SW3 5BS

Copyright © Editorial LIBSA, Narciso Serra, 25 – Tel 433 54 07 –
28007 MADRID
4.ª EDICION 1991
Copyright English language text © 1993 Sunburst Books

ISBN 1 85778 004 3

Printed and bound in China

ENTERTAINING

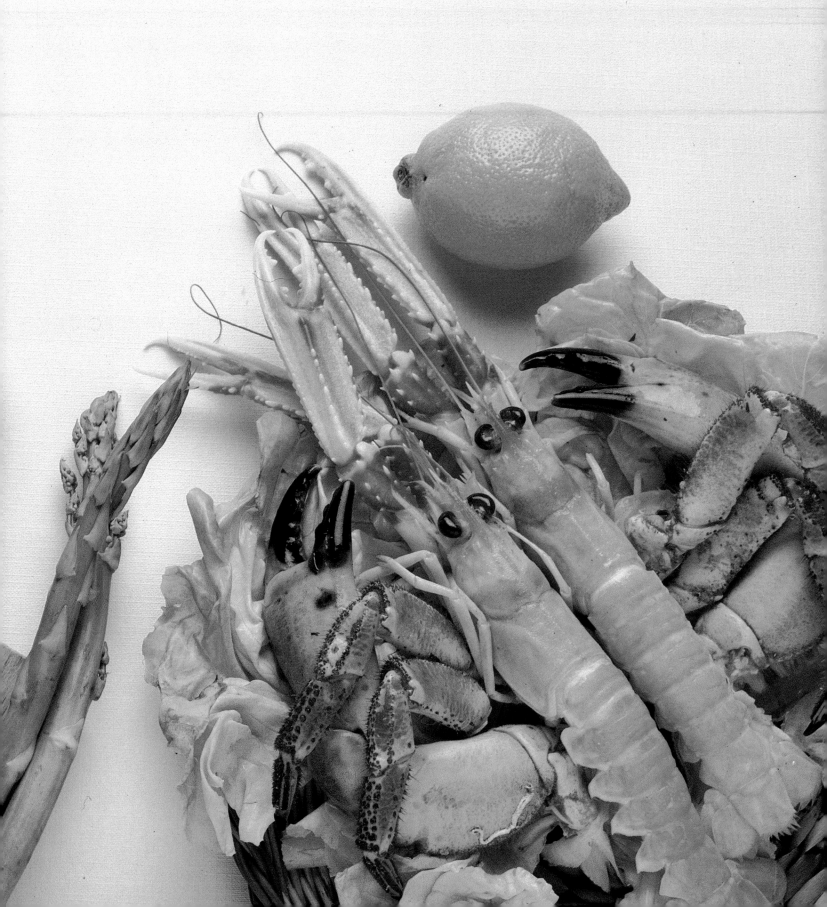

CONTENTS

INTRODUCTION

Every cook's repertoire of recipes should include a few dishes for the special occasions which arise from time to time. Almost all festivities or celebrations tend to revolve around a meal of some sort, whether it be Christmas dinner, lunch on Easter Sunday or a family anniversary.

These events are anticipated with great excitement by all the guests, and, often, with great trepidation by the host or hostess responsible for providing the special meal to fulfil these expectations.

This book presents the solution for anxious cooks faced with the prospect of entertaining. *Entertaining* contains a broad range of recipes suited to every occasion, from silver and golden wedding anniversaries and dinner parties to cold buffets and light lunch or supper dishes for informal gatherings of family and friends.

The book is packed with ideas for starters, main courses and desserts, as well as recipes for festive cakes and pastries, and numerous tips on presentation and accompaniments for particular dishes.

When preparing party food, whatever the occasion, it is important to consider the colour and texture of the combination of dishes on your menu as well as the individual dishes. But it is also essential to be realistic and to assess carefully the time and resources at your disposal to create your special meal. The key is to keep it as simple as possible and to plan ahead to ensure that everything runs smoothly whilst appearing to be no effort on your part. The sign of a successful party is not just good food, but good food served by a relaxed host or hostess.

CHRISTMAS

PRAWN STUFFED EGGS

Serves 6

12 hard-boiled eggs, shelled
100 g/3¹/₂ oz cooked prawns in their shells
2 tbsp chopped parsley
3 tbsp flour
1 egg, beaten
1 onion, peeled and finely chopped
2 garlic cloves, finely chopped
oil for frying
salt
pepper

Cut the eggs in half, remove the yolks and place in a mixing bowl.

Peel the prawns, reserving the shells, and mash together with the egg yolks and half the chopped parsley to form a paste. Stuff the egg whites with this mixture. Dredge them in 2 tbsp flour, coat with the beaten egg, then chill. Drain them and arrange in an ovenproof dish.

Meanwhile, boil the prawn shells in a little water for 10 minutes, drain, reserving the cooking liquid, and mash in a mortar. Strain the reserved liquid and set aside. Preheat the oven to 170° C/325° F, gas mark 3. Sauté the onion and garlic in a little oil, add the remaining flour and stir well. Stir in the reserved liquid, simmer for a few minutes then season with salt and pepper. Strain and pour over the eggs. Place in the oven for 30 minutes. Sprinkle over the remaining parsley and serve straight from the dish.

CASTILLIAN ROAST LAMB

Serves 6

1 boned leg of lamb
2 sprigs oregano
1 tsp salt
60 g/2 oz butter
2 garlic cloves, finely chopped
250 g/9 oz onions, peeled and finely chopped
1 tbsp chopped parsley
¹/₂ tsp ground cloves
100 ml/3¹/₂ fl oz white wine

Make a few gashes in the meat. Pound 1 sprig oregano with the salt and rub into the lamb, then rub with the butter. Pound together the garlic, onion, parsley, cloves and the remaining oregano, add the wine and an equal amount of water. Pour this mixture over the lamb and leave to marinate for 3 hours. Preheat the oven to 180° C/350° F, gas mark 4 and roast the lamb for 30 minutes per 500 g/1 lb, basting occasionally. Best served with courgettes.

RED CABBAGE CASSEROLE

Serves 5

4 tbsp oil
500 g/1 lb 2 oz onions, peeled and chopped
100 g/3¹/₂ oz Serrano ham or coppa, chopped
100 g/3¹/₂ oz bacon, derinded and chopped

Top: Prawn Stuffed Eggs
Bottom: Castillian Roast Lamb

1 red cabbage, finely chopped
250 ml/9 fl oz red wine
salt
white pepper
100 g/3½ oz frankfurters
60 g/2 oz pine nuts, roasted

Heat the oil in a casserole, add the onion, ham and bacon, and cook for 10 minutes. Add the cabbage, red wine, seasoning and a little water. Cover and allow to stew for 1 hour. When the cabbage is cooked, slice the frankfurters into small pieces and add them, together with the roasted pine nuts. Serve at once.

VERMICELLI FISH SOUP

Serves 6

200 g/7 oz prawns, peeled, shells reserved
4 tbsp oil
5 garlic cloves, chopped
100 ml/3½ fl oz fresh tomato sauce
1 tbsp flour
100 ml/3½ fl oz white wine
1 tbsp chopped parsley
salt
white pepper
200 g/7 oz squid, cut into strips
225 g/8 oz vermicelli
450 ml/15 fl oz hot fish stock

Put the prawn shells in a small pan, add just enough water to cover, simmer for 10 minutes, then strain. Heat the oil, sauté the chopped garlic and add the tomato sauce, flour, wine, parsley, salt and pepper, prawns and squid. Add the prawn shell stock and cook for 10 minutes. Add the vermicelli and hot fish stock and cook for a further 12 minutes. Add more stock if necessary.

CHAMPAGNE CAPON

Serves 8-10

1 kg/2¼ lb apples
1 capon or large chicken
250 g/9 oz pitted prunes, chopped
1 tsp salt
100 g/3½ oz lard
2 garlic cloves, finely chopped
½ bottle champagne or sparkling wine
75 ml/2½ fl oz single cream

2 tbsp sherry
2 tsp lemon juice
120 g/4 oz butter
250 g/9 oz button mushrooms

Preheat the oven to 200° C/400° F, gas mark 6. Peel, core and chop the apples. Reserve the peel. Stuff the capon or chicken with the chopped apples and prunes, and rub over salt and most of the

lard. Heat the remaining lard in a casserole, add the garlic, then brown the capon all over. Cook in the oven for 10 minutes, then pour over the wine. Reduce the oven temperature to 180° C/350° F, gas mark 4. Cover the casserole and return to the oven for about 2 hours or until the capon or is tender. Place on a heated

Top: Red Cabbage Casserole
Bottom: Vermicelli Fish Soup

serving dish. Strain the sauce and add the cream. Season and keep warm in a bain-marie.

Place the apple peelings in a saucepan with the sherry, half the lemon juice and half the butter. Cover and simmer for 15 minutes until tender then liquidize. In a separate pan, cook the mushrooms in the remaining butter and enough water to cover. Season with salt and the remaining lemon juice and simmer for 5 minutes. Drain.

Serve the capon garnished with the apple purée and mushrooms and hand the sauce separately in a jug.

STUFFED SEA BREAM

Serves 6

1 sea bream, about 2 kg/4½ lb
250 g/9 oz peeled prawns
150 g/5 oz Serrano ham or coppa, chopped
2 hard-boiled eggs, shelled and chopped
juice of 1 lemon
1 tbsp chopped parsley
salt and pepper
6 tbsp oil
2 tomatoes, thinly sliced
2 onions, peeled and thinly sliced
100 ml/3½ fl oz white wine

Ask your fishmonger to clean the bream, removing the backbone but leaving the head. Prepare the stuffing by mixing together the prawns, ham and eggs. Add half the lemon juice, half the parsley and 2 tbsp of the oil, mix well then stuff the bream with this mixture.

Preheat the oven to 230° C/450° F, gas mark 8. Put 2 tbsp of the oil in a large ovenproof dish. Arrange the sliced tomato and onion in the base, and place the bream on top. Add the remaining oil and lemon juice, and the wine. Cook in the oven for 30 minutes.

Place the bream on a serving dish, garnish with the sauce and serve with sautéed potatoes sprinkled with the remaining parsley.

NEW YEAR'S EVE CAKE

Serves 8

200 g/7 oz sugar
6 eggs, beaten
200 g/7 oz flour

For the cream filling:
75 ml/2½ fl oz water
100 g/3½ oz sugar
3 egg yolks

For the icing:
120 g/4 oz icing sugar
few drops of lemon juice
1 egg white

For decoration:
melted chocolate
sliced oranges
grapes, halved and pips removed

Preheat the oven to 180° C/350° F, gas mark 4. Place the sugar in a mixing bowl and gradually beat in the eggs. Fold in the flour, and pour into a greased cake tin. Bake in the oven for about 30 minutes. Cool on a wire rack.

Lower the oven temperature to 140° C/275° F, gas mark ½.

For the filling, heat the water and sugar together to make a thin syrup. While this is still hot, pour over the yolks and cook for a few minutes, stirring all the time. Cut the cake in half horizontally and fill with this mixture.

For the icing, stir all the ingredients together to make a thin white cream. Spread over the top of the cake and return to the oven to allow it to dry. Decorate with melted chocolate to make a clock. Garnish with sliced oranges and grapes.

CHRISTMAS EVE RING

Serves 8

250 g/9 oz butter
200 g/7 oz sugar
4 eggs
grated rind of 1 lemon
350 g/12 oz flour
60 ml/2 fl oz milk

For the biscuits:
120 g/4 oz flour
45 g/1½ oz sugar
75 g/2½ oz butter
few drops of vanilla essence

For the glaze:
120 g/4 oz icing sugar
1 egg white
few drops of lemon juice

Preheat the oven to 180° C/350° F, gas mark 4. Cream the butter in a mixing bowl, add the sugar a little at a time, then add the eggs one by one, and finally the lemon rind, sifted flour and milk. Pour into a buttered, floured ring mould and bake in the oven for 40 minutes.

Decorate with piped cream or alternatively with glazed biscuits and a red candle, tied with silver ribbon.

Preheat the oven to 180° C/350° F, gas mark 4. To make the biscuits, place the flour on a board. Make a well in the centre and add the remaining ingredients. Knead together until the dough is no longer sticky. Roll out, and cut into shapes: half-moons, stars and rounds. Bake in the oven for 20 minutes.

To make the glaze, beat all the ingredients together to form a stiff, white cream. Add colouring to taste, coat the biscuits and dry briefly in a low oven.

CHESTNUT CAKE

Serves 8

6 eggs
200 g/7 oz sugar
200 g/7 oz flour

For the chestnut icing:
100 ml/3½ fl oz water
200 g/7 oz sugar
1 x large can chestnut purée
150 g/5 oz butter, softened
60 ml/2 fl oz Kirsch

For the topping:
120 g/4 oz chocolate
60 g/2 oz butter

Preheat the oven to 180° C/350° F, gas mark 4. Beat together the eggs and sugar, until thick and creamy. Sift in the flour and stir carefully. Turn into a buttered and floured round cake tin and bake in the oven for 30 minutes.

Put the water in a saucepan over low heat, add the sugar and stir occasionally until a syrup forms. Remove from the heat and, while still warm, stir in the chestnut purée, softened butter and Kirsch. Slice the cake in half, fill with half the chestnut cream, then use the rest to cover the sides. Melt the chocolate and butter together and use to ice the top.

Christmas Eve Ring

HOLY WEEK AND EASTER DISHES

ROAST LAMB

Serves 4

1 rack of lamb
salt
75 g/2¹/₂ oz lard
5 garlic cloves
60 ml/2 fl oz white wine
60 ml/2 fl oz water
500 g/1 lb 2 oz potatoes, peeled, cubed and
sautéed

Preheat the oven to 180° C/350° F, gas
mark 4. Rub the lamb all over with salt.
Heat the lard in a casserole and fry the
garlic until lightly coloured. Add the lamb
and roast in the oven for 30 minutes per
500 g/1 lb 2 oz. Remove the lamb to a
heated serving dish. Add the wine and
water to the casserole and bring to the
boil. Pour into a gravy boat. Surround the
lamb with the hot sautéed potatoes and
serve with a lettuce and tomato salad.

EASTER CAKE WITH MERINGUE ROSES

Serves 6

For the sponge:
6 eggs
200 g/7 oz sugar
200 g/7 oz flour
150 ml/5 fl oz light syrup
250 g/9 oz apricot jam

For the icing:
150 g/5 oz sugar
100 ml/ 3¹/₂ fl oz water
4 egg yolks, beaten

For the roses:
6 egg whites
250 g/9 oz castor sugar
1 tbsp cornflour
few drops of vinegar

For the decoration:
6 confectionery chocolate eggs
100 g/3¹/₂ oz chocolate, grated

Preheat the oven to 190° C/375° F, gas
mark 5. Make a sponge by beating
together the eggs and sugar over a pan of
hot water. Fold in the flour, turn into a
cake tin and bake in the oven for 30

minutes. Soak with some syrup, then cut
in half and fill with apricot jam.
    For the icing, simmer together the sugar
and water until a syrup forms. Add to the
egg yolks in a bain-marie and cook,
stirring, until thickened. Cool, then use to
ice the sponge.
    Preheat the oven to 120° C/250° F, gas
mark ¹/₂. For the meringue roses, beat the
egg whites until stiff, gradually adding the
sugar. Fold in the cornflour and vinegar
and place teaspoonsful on a baking sheet
lined with greaseproof paper. Bake in the
oven for about 45 minutes. Allow to cool,
then assemble into 'rose' shapes, using
apricot jam to hold each cluster of
meringue 'roses' together. Place the roses
on the cake, decorate the cake with
chocolate eggs and grated chocolate then
tie with a ribbon.

SALT COD BRANDADE

Serves 4

500 g/1 lb 2 oz salt cod
120 g/4 oz butter
1 tbsp lemon juice
150 g/5 oz potatoes, peeled
100 ml/3¹/₂ fl oz oil
250 ml/9 fl oz thick Béchamel sauce
150 ml/5 fl oz cream
salt
pepper

Cut the salt cod into large pieces and soak
for 24 hours in cold water, changing the
water 3 times. Drain and poach in
simmering water for 20 minutes. Drain
again, allow to cool, then flake the flesh,
removing the bones. Place in a saucepan
with the butter and lemon juice and heat
gently until the butter is absorbed.
    Meanwhile, boil and purée the potatoes
then gradually add the oil, a little at a time,
as if making mayonnaise. Add to the
thickened Béchamel sauce and heat gently,
stirring all the time. Gradually add the
cream and season with salt and pepper.
Serve piled in a pyramid shape on a round
dish, garnished with slices of fried bread
and fresh tomato sauce, if desired.

FRIED BREAD IN WHITE WINE

Serves 8

1 loaf white bread, thickly sliced
1 litre/1³/₄ pints white wine
250 g/9 oz sugar
rind of 1 orange, cut into strips
rind of 1 lemon, cut into strips
2 eggs, beaten
1 tbsp cinnamon

Use slightly stale bread, as it does not
become soggy when soaked. Lay the bread
slices in a shallow dish. Boil the wine with
half the sugar and the strips of orange and
lemon rind. Pour the hot mixture over the
bread. Drain and coat in beaten egg, then
fry in very hot oil.
    Allow to cool, then sprinkle them with
the remaining sugar mixed with the
cinnamon.

FRIED EGGS WITH CROUTONS AND CHORIZO

Serves 6

1 small loaf of day-old white bread, sliced
salt
oil for frying
3 garlic cloves
6 eggs
150 g/5 oz chorizo sausage, sliced into 6 pieces

Remove the crusts from the bread slices,
then cube the bread. Arrange the cubes on
a teacloth and sprinkle with water, shaking
the cloth so that they are equally
moistened. Season with salt and leave to
rest for a while.
    Heat enough oil in a frying-pan to fry
the bread. First fry the garlic cloves until
golden then remove. Fry the bread cubes
for about 10 minutes, first on a high heat,
lowering it towards the end.
    Heat some more oil in the pan and
gently fry the eggs and sliced chorizo,
turning once. Arrange the croûtons on a
pyramid on a dish, with the eggs around
them and the chorizo on top.

Top: Roast Lamb
Bottom: Salt Cod Brandade

GARLIC LAMB

Serves 5

1½ kg/3¼ lb leg of lamb, boned
75 g/2½ oz lard
60 g/2 oz garlic, chopped
1 tbsp breadcrumbs
300 ml/10 fl oz fresh tomato sauce
250 ml/9 fl oz boiling water
salt and pepper
500 ml/18 fl oz meat stock

Cut the lamb into 6.5 cm/2½ inch cubes, or larger slices. Heat the lard in a casserole, add the garlic, and brown the meat all over. Add the breadcrumbs, tomato sauce, boiling water, salt and pepper. Cover and cook over a low heat until tender, about 1½ hours. Throughout the cooking time add the stock a little at a time to moisten as required.

Arrange the meat on a serving dish and pour over the sauce. Serve with sauté potatoes or boiled white rice.

COD CASSEROLE

Serves 6

500 g/1 lb 2 oz cod
1 kg/2¼ lb potatoes, peeled
1 kg/2¼ lb tomatoes, skinned, seeded and sliced
250 g/9 oz onions, peeled and sliced
3 tbsp olive oil
1 garlic clove, chopped
Salt and pepper

Cut the cod into medium sized pieces.
Cut the potatoes into small pieces. Arrange the potatoes, tomatoes, onions and fish in layers in a casserole, adding a little oil and salt and pepper to each layer. Dry-fry the garlic and sprinkle over the dish. Cover and cook on a low heat for 1 hour until tender.

COD, CHICKPEA AND SPINACH STEW

Serves 4

250 g/9 oz cod
500 g/1 lb 2 oz chickpeas
3 tbsp oil
2 onions, peeled and chopped
2 garlic cloves, peeled and chopped
1 tbsp chopped parsley
100 g/3½ oz bread, thinly sliced
1 hard-boiled egg, shelled and finely chopped
250 g/9 oz spinach
salt

Cut the cod into medium sized pieces.
Soak the chickpeas in warm water for 24 hours. Place in a casserole with 1 tablespoon of oil and cook over a very low heat until tender.

Meanwhile, sauté the chopped onion, garlic, parsley and bread slices in the remaining oil. Add the chopped egg. Boil and drain the spinach and add to the chickpeas when they are almost done. Stir in the salt cod and sautéed onion mixture. Stir well and cook for a further 15 minutes. Season with salt.

If you prefer a thicker sauce, sieve or liquidize a few chickpeas and stir them into the stew. Serve sprinkled with extra chopped hard-boiled eggs, if desired.

EASTER CAKE WITH PRALINE CREAM

Serves 6

For the sponge:
7 eggs
225 g/8 oz sugar
225 g/8 oz flour
icing sugar for dusting

For the praline cream:
2 eggs
6 tbsp plus 100 g/3½ oz sugar
1 tsp cocoa powder
100 g/3½ oz almonds, toasted
150 g/5 oz butter, softened

Grated plain chocolate to decorate

Preheat the oven to 180° C/350° F, gas mark 4. For the sponge, beat together the eggs and sugar then fold in the flour. Turn into a buttered and floured cake tin, and bake in the oven for 30 minutes until firm.

For the cream, beat the eggs in a heatproof mixing bowl with the 6 tbsp sugar for 10 minutes. Place the bowl over a pan of simmering water and cook, stirring, for 20 minutes. Add the cocoa powder and remove from the heat. Melt the remaining sugar in a pan with a little water then boil until golden and pour over the nuts. Cool, then crush to a powder with a rolling pin. Add the softened butter to the cooled cream, then stir in the nut praline.

Cut the cake in half horizontally, and use half of the praline cream to sandwich the two layers of cake together. Spread the remaining cream over the cake and decorate with grated plain chocolate.

Top: Cod Casserole
Bottom: Garlic Lamb

ROAST LAMB WITH MILANESE RICE

Serves 8

100 g/3½ oz lard
2 kg/4½ lb lamb, best end of neck
salt and pepper
2 onions, peeled and finely chopped
2 leeks, trimmed and finely chopped
2 celery stalks, finely chopped
2 tsp chopped parsley
75 ml/2½ fl oz Madeira
1 kg/2¼ lb spinach
100 g/3½ oz butter
250 g/9 oz cooked rice
250 g/9 oz cheese, grated
8 cherry tomatoes, grilled

Preheat the oven to 180° C/350° F, gas mark 4. Melt the lard in a large casserole dish. Season the lamb with salt and pepper and brown in the hot lard. Remove, and cook the onions, leeks, celery and parsley. Place the meat on top of the cooked vegetables and roast in the oven for about 1¾ hours, basting occasionally. Remove the lamb and bone it. Strain the cooking juices and add the Madeira to make a gravy.

Meanwhile, make the Milanese rice. Boil and drain the spinach then sauté in the butter. Stir in the cooked rice and half the cheese. Arrange the rice on a serving dish, place the lamb on top and garnish with the remaining cheese and grilled tomatoes. Serve the gravy in a sauceboat.

BROAD BEAN STEW

Serves 6

250 ml/9 fl oz oil
500 g/1 lb 2 oz onions, peeled and chopped
3 garlic cloves, chopped
1½ kg/3¼ lb shelled broad beans
salt
100 ml/3½ fl oz wine
200 g/7 oz Serrano ham or coppa, diced
1 tsp paprika
1 slice white bread, fried

Heat the oil and fry the onion and garlic until softened. Meanwhile, simmer the beans in salted water until barely tender. Drain and add to the onions with the salt,

Left: Broad Bean Stew
Right: Eggs with Asparagus

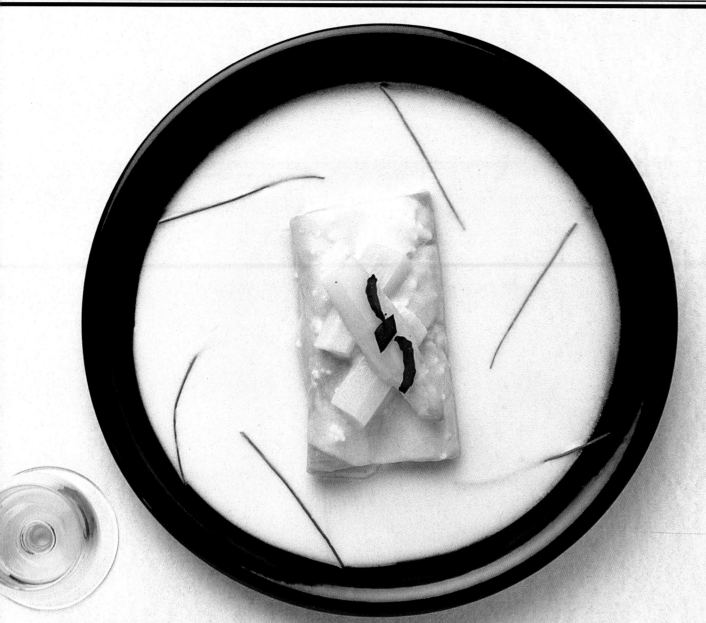

wine, ham and just enough water to cover and cook for a further 15 minutes. Crumble over the fried bread and cook for a few more minutes. Serve with chips.

COD WITH PEPPERS

Serves 6

500 g/1 lb 2 oz cod
1 kg/2¼ lb red peppers, halved, seeds removed
2 tbsp olive oil
500 g/1 lb 2 oz onions, peeled and sliced
500 g/1 lb 2 oz potatoes, peeled and diced
3 eggs, beaten

Place the cod in a saucepan and add enough water to cover. Bring to the boil and simmer for 5 minutes. Drain and flake the fish, discarding the bones. Fry the peppers in oil, peel and cut them into strips. Fry the onions until softened, add the strips of pepper and simmer over low heat until it becomes very thick. Fry the cubed potatoes and mix into the onions and peppers, then add the fish. Add the

beaten eggs and cook over a low heat until thickened. Serve garnished with fried bread.

EGGS WITH ASPARAGUS

Serves 6

500 g/1 lb 2 oz asparagus, trimmed
1 tbsp oil
1 onion, peeled and chopped
salt and pepper
60 g/2 oz butter
1 tbsp flour
3 egg yolks
150 ml/5 fl oz cream
6 eggs, poached
6 slices York ham
1 hard-boiled egg, shelled and chopped
1 truffle, finely sliced

Place the asparagus in a large pan, add the oil, onion, salt and pepper. Pour on enough boiling water to cover, then simmer for 10 minutes until tender. Drain, reserving the liquid, and purée the

asparagus, reserving a few tips for garnish.

To make the sauce, melt the butter, stir in the flour and cook for 2 minutes. Stir in the asparagus water, puréed asparagus, egg yolks and cream. Season and keep warm.

Arrange the poached eggs on the slices of ham and roll up. Arrange on a serving dish and pour over the sauce. Garnish with the reserved asparagus tips, chopped egg and truffle.

LENTEN BUNS

Serves 10

100 g/3¹/₂ oz flour
75 g/2¹/₂ oz fresh yeast
warm water as necessary
60 ml/2 fl oz oil
pinch salt
30 g/1 oz sugar
3 tbsp currants, soaked and drained
300 g/10 oz candied orange peel, diced
30 g/1 oz pine nuts
30 g/1 oz icing sugar

Place half the flour in a mixing bowl and crumble in the yeast. Add warm water, a little at a time, until you achieve a dough you can knead. Cover with a cloth and leave to stand in a warm place until the dough has doubled in size (about 20 minutes).

Place the remaining flour in a circle on a board, and put the oil, salt and risen dough in the centre. Add warm water then knead firmly until the mixture becomes quite soft and no longer sticks to your fingers. Now add the sugar, work it in well, sprinkle with a little flour, cover with a cloth and leave for about 1 hour to rise again.

Work the currants, orange peel and pine nuts into the risen dough. Divide into 10 buns, arrange on a baking tray and leave to double in size (40 minutes to 1 hour).

Meanwhile, preheat the oven to 190° C/375° F, gas mark 5. Bake the buns in the oven for 15–20 minutes and leave to cool. Mix the icing sugar with a little water to make a glacé icing and use to coat the buns. Return the buns briefly to the oven to dry the icing.

COD PILAFF

Serves 4

200 g/7 oz cod
2 potatoes, peeled and finely sliced
60 g/2 oz French beans, diced
60 g/2 oz shelled peas
60 g/2 oz canned artichoke hearts, sliced
2 small red peppers, diced
1 garlic clove, chopped
1 tbsp chopped parsley
1 tsp tomato purée
¹/₄ tsp paprika
¹/₄ tsp saffron
250 g/9 oz rice, boiled and drained

Place the cod in a saucepan and add enough water to cover. Bring to the boil and simmer for 5 minutes. Preheat the oven to 220° C/425° F, gas mark 7. Drain and flake the fish, discarding any bones. Sauté the vegetables with chopped garlic and parsley, stir in a little tomato purée and paprika. Combine with the rice and cod in an ovenproof dish. Pour on the saffron mixed with a little boiling water, cover and cook in the oven for 20 minutes.

Left, top: Cod Pilaff
Left, bottom: Lenten Buns
Opposite, top: Hake Basque style
Opposite, bottom: Steak in Green Peppercorn Sauce

SILVER AND GOLDEN WEDDING ANNIVERSARIES

HAKE BASQUE STYLE

Serves 6

750 g/1½ lb clams
1 kg/2¼ lb hake or cod steaks
salt and pepper
6 tbsp olive oil
6 garlic cloves, chopped
1 tbsp chopped parsley
150 g/5 oz peas, cooked
200 g/7 oz canned asparagus, drained and chopped
2 hard-boiled eggs, shelled and halved

Wash the clams thoroughly under cold running water, discarding any which do not close when sharply tapped. Place in a saucepan, cover with cold water and boil, discarding any which do not open. Remove from the heat and strain through muslin, reserving the stock.

Season the hake steaks with salt and pepper. Heat the oil in a large frying-pan and sauté the garlic and hake, shaking the pan frequently to release the thickening properties of the gelatine in the skin of the fish. Add the reserved clam stock, or a little fish stock, parsley and peas, continuing to shake the pan until the sauce has thickened. Garnish with asparagus, the clams and eggs.

STEAK IN GREEN PEPPERCORN SAUCE

Serves 6

4 tbsp oil
6 slices fillet steak
2 onions, peeled and finely chopped
350 g/12 oz button mushrooms, sliced
8 tbsp white wine
8 tbsp fresh tomato sauce
salt
1 tbsp green peppercorns
150 ml/5 fl oz strained yoghurt

Heat the oil in a large frying-pan and quickly brown the steaks over high heat, turning once. Remove the meat and set aside. Add the onions, mushrooms, wine and fresh tomato sauce to the pan, season with salt, then simmer for 15 minutes. Replace the meat, add the green peppercorns and cook for a further 5 minutes, or until the meat is tender.

Remove from the heat and stir in the yoghurt. Serve garnished with lemon slices, if desired.

CARAMELIZED PINEAPPLE

Serves 6

8 slices fresh pineapple

60 g/2 oz butter
2 tbsp demerara sugar
100 g/3½ fl oz pineapple juice
8 tbsp Kirsch
100 g/3½ oz mixed crystallized fruit, finely chopped
½ tsp cinnamon

Preheat the oven to 180° C/350° F, gas mark 4. Arrange the pineapple in an

ovenproof dish. Simmer the butter, sugar, pineapple juice and Kirsch to make a syrup, then pour over the pineapple. Sprinkle with the chopped fruit and cinnamon. Cook in the oven for about 10 minutes and serve at room temperature.

STACKED OMELETTES

Serves 6

2 large onions, peeled and finely chopped
1 tbsp oil
500 g/1 lb 2 oz spinach
120 g/4 oz butter
9 eggs
salt
3 tbsp milk or single cream
200 g/7 oz Serrano ham or coppa, cut into strips
225 ml/8 fl oz fresh tomato sauce
150 g/5 oz canned asparagus tips

Sauté the onions in a little oil until soft and golden. Boil the spinach briefly, drain well and sauté in 30 g/1 oz butter. Remove from heat and set aside.

Make an omelette as follows. Beat 3 eggs together with salt and 1 tbsp milk or single cream. Heat 30 g/1 oz butter in a frying-pan, preferably non-stick. Raise the heat and pour in the beaten eggs. Stir with a fork, drawing the edges to the centre as they begin to set. When cooked, slide on to a warm plate. Make 2 more omelettes in the same way. Layer the omelettes with the mixture of the onions, spinach and ham on a heated serving dish, then pour the hot tomato sauce over the stack.

Different fillings may be used: chopped cooked artichoke hearts, mushrooms, chicken, prawns, etc. You may also wish to cover the omelettes with a different sauce, e.g. Béchamel, and sprinkle with grated cheese and briefly grill them. Garnish the stack with asparagus tips.

MONKFISH WITH PRAWNS IN BRANDY

Serves 5

2 tbsp flour
750 g/1½ lb monkfish fillets, cut into bite-size pieces
60 g/2 oz butter
1 tbsp oil
350 g/12 oz cooked, peeled prawns
1 onion, peeled and chopped
6 tbsp fresh tomato sauce
60 ml/2 fl oz white wine
4 tbsp brandy
225 ml/8 fl oz fish stock

salt
pepper
8 tbsp single cream

Roll the monkfish pieces in seasoned flour and fry them in the butter and a little oil until golden. Place in a flameproof casserole with the prawns. In the same frying-pan, sauté the chopped onion for 2 minutes, then add the tomato sauce, wine, brandy and stock. Season with salt and pepper and simmer for 10 minutes. Strain, add the cream and pour over the fish. Simmer for 10 minutes then serve with white rice.

CHESTNUT PUDDING

Serves 6

750 g/1½ lb chestnuts
100 ml/3½ fl oz milk
8 tbsp brandy
3 eggs, beaten
100 g/3½ oz sugar
150 g/5 oz sponge cake, crumbled
100 g/3½ oz walnuts, finely chopped
200 ml/7 fl oz whipping cream

Score the chestnuts, boil for a few minutes then drain and peel off the skin. Place in a saucepan with the milk and brandy and simmer for 30 minutes until tender. Remove from the heat and mash with the eggs, sugar, sponge cake and chopped walnuts. Pour the mixture into a buttered cake tin. Place in a bain-marie and cook in the oven for 45 minutes. When cold, turn out on to a serving dish. Beat the cream and use to decorate the cake. Serve with a chocolate sauce, if desired.

CHICKEN MOUSSELINE

Serves 8

1 x 1.25 kg/2¾ lb chicken
1 onion, peeled and quartered
1 leek, roughly chopped
1 celery stalk, roughly chopped
100 g/3½ oz liver sausage
8 tbsp double or whipping cream
4 tbsp port
4 tbsp brandy
salt
pepper
6 tbsp liquid gelatine

Place the chicken in a flameproof casserole. Add the onion, leek and celery and just enough water to cover the chicken. Cover and simmer for 1¼ hours until tender. Drain the chicken and

remove skin and bones. Purée the breasts with the liver sausage, cream, port and brandy and season with salt and pepper. If the mixture is too thick, add a little of the cooking liquid. Stir in the cooked gelatine and pour into a wetted mould. Chill in the refrigerator for 1 hour or until set.

SEVILLE TUNA

Serves 4

4 x 150 g/ 5 oz tuna steaks
salt
pepper
1 tbsp flour
4 tbsp oil
1 onion, peeled and finely chopped
60 ml/2 fl oz white wine
1 tbsp vinegar
1 bayleaf
350 g/12 oz ripe tomatoes, skinned, seeded and chopped
1 tbsp chopped parsley
200 g/7 oz green and black olives
4 small gherkins, sliced

Coat the tuna steaks in seasoned flour and brown them in the hot oil. Remove the tuna steaks. Sauté the onion in the same oil. Stir in any remaining flour and add the wine, vinegar, bayleaf and tomatoes. Return the tuna steaks to the pan and add enough water to cover the fish. Season with salt, pepper and parsley. Cover and simmer for about 45 minutes. Remove the tuna, arrange on a serving dish and keep warm. Simmer the sauce a further 10 minutes, add the olives and gherkins and pour over the fish.

POTATO FLAN

Serves 5

250 g/9 oz potatoes, peeled
1 medium cauliflower
3 eggs
100 ml/3½ fl oz milk, warmed
8 tbsp mayonnaise
1 tbsp chopped parsley
salt and pepper
30 g/1 oz butter

Boil the potatoes for 15 minutes, drain and slice finely. Divide the cauliflower into florets, boil for 15 minutes then drain. Layer the potatoes and cauliflower in individual ovenproof dishes.

Top: Seville Tuna
Bottom: Potato Flan

Preheat the oven to 180 ° C/350 ° F, gas mark 4. Beat together the eggs, warmed milk, mayonnaise, parsley, salt and pepper and pour over the vegetables. Dot with the butter and bake in the oven for 10 minutes.

COURGETTES STUFFED WITH PRAWNS

Serves 5

5 medium courgettes, halved lengthways
salt
pepper
100 g/3½ oz tuna
250 g/9 oz cooked shelled prawns, chopped
60 g/2 oz olives, chopped
500 ml/18 fl oz fresh tomato sauce
2 tbsp dried breadcrumbs

Left: Courgettes Stuffed with Prawns
Right: Pheasant with Grapes

Seed the courgette halves and boil for 10 minutes in salted water. Preheat the oven to 180° C/350° F, gas mark 4. Crumble the tuna and mix with the prawns, olives, pepper and a few tablespoons of the tomato sauce. Fill the courgettes with this mixture. Spoon some of the remaining tomato sauce into an ovenproof dish, then lay the stuffed courgettes on top. Spoon over the remaining tomato sauce and sprinkle with breadcrumbs. Cook in the oven for 12 minutes.

PHEASANT WITH GRAPES

Serves 8
100 g/3½ oz lard
8 tbsp oil
2 pheasants, plucked and drawn
500 g/l lb 2 oz onions, peeled and sliced
1 kg/2¼ lb seedless grapes, peeled
250 ml/9 fl oz white wine
250 ml/9 fl oz single cream
salt
pepper

Heat the lard and oil in a flameproof casserole and brown the pheasants on all sides. Add the onions and grapes. When the onions begin to brown, add the wine and a little water or stock. Cover and cook on a low heat for about 1½ hours until tender.

Remove the pheasants, cut in half and arrange in a fairly deep, warmed serving dish. Heat the cooking liquid in the casserole, stir in the cream and season with salt and pepper. Pour over the pheasant pieces and serve.

BIRTHDAY DISHES

LAMB CHOPS WITH BECHAMEL SAUCE

Serves 4

8 lamb chops
salt
pepper
oil for frying
75 g/2¹/₂ oz butter

170-225 g/6-8 oz flour
500 ml/18 fl oz milk, warmed
1 egg, beaten
120 g/4 oz dried breadcrumbs
Garnish:
8 tomatoes, grilled (optional)

Season the chops with salt and pepper, then fry briefly on both sides in hot oil. Drain well.

Make the Béchamel sauce: melt the butter, stir in 2 tablespoons of flour then slowly add the warm milk, stirring all the time, season with salt and pepper, and simmer until thickened. Coat the chops with the sauce and arrange them on a lightly oiled plate.

Allow to cool and coat in the remaining flour. Then coat with beaten egg and breadcrumbs. Fry until golden in plenty of very hot oil, drain, arrange them on a long dish and garnish with grilled tomatoes, if desired.

TUNA ASALMONADO PIE

Serves 6

45 g/1¹/₂ oz butter
30 g/1 oz flour
250 ml/9 fl oz milk
1 kg/2¹/₄ lb canned tuna
250 ml/9 fl oz fresh tomato sauce
4 eggs
salt and white pepper
200 g/7 oz asparagus tips
100 g/3¹/₂ oz olives
1 tomato, thinly sliced

Make a thick Béchamel sauce (see previous recipe) with the butter, flour and milk. Place the tuna in a mixing bowl and mash with a fork. Add the Béchamel and the tomato sauce, then the eggs, one by one, mixing together thoroughly after each ingredient is added. Season with salt and pepper. Butter a ring mould and fill with the mixture. Place in a bain-marie and cook in the oven for about 20 minutes. Remove, allow to rest and turn out on to a serving dish. Garnish with the asparagus tips, olives and sliced tomato.

ALMOND CHARLOTTE

Serves 8

30 sponge fingers
100 g/¹/₂ oz butter

**Left, above: Tuna Asalmonado Pie
Left, bottom:Chicken Mousseline
Opposite, above: Almond Charlotte
Opposite, bottom: Lamb Chops in
Béchamel Sauce**

the oven for about 30 minutes or until the top springs back when lightly pressed. Turn out on to a wire rack and cool.

To make the cream, simmer the sugar with the water for 5 minutes until a syrup forms. Add the egg yolks, softened butter, instant coffee and beat until the coffee is dissolved.

Slice the sponge in half, and fill with half the mocha cream. Cover the top and sides with the remaining cream. Sprinkle with toasted almond flakes, if desired. Chill before serving.

LOBSTER AU GRATIN WITH CHAMPAGNE

Serves 6

1 lobster
1 bayleaf
salt and pepper
500 g/1 lb 2 oz Dublin Bay prawns, cooked
1 onion, peeled and diced

200 g/7 oz icing sugar
few drops of vanilla essence
60 ml/2 fl oz Kirsch
200 g/7 oz almonds, chopped
300 ml/10 fl oz whipping cream
8 glacé cherries

Lightly butter a charlotte mould and line with sponge fingers, reserving some for the top. Trim the fingers to fit.

To make the filling, put the butter in a mixing bowl and beat to soften. Gradually beat in the icing sugar until light and creamy. Stir in the vanilla essence, Kirsch and chopped almonds. Beat the cream and fold in. Fill the mould with this mixture and arrange a layer of sponge fingers on the top. Chill thoroughly, turn out of the mould and serve garnished with glacé cherries.

MOCHA CAKE

Serves 6

For the sponge:
3 eggs
100 g/3½ oz sugar
100 g/3½ oz flour

For the mocha cream:
200 g/7 oz sugar
75 ml/2½ fl oz water
2 egg yolks
250 g/9 oz butter, softened
1 tbsp instant coffee

toasted almond flakes (optional)

To make the sponge, beat together the eggs and sugar, then fold in the flour a little at a time. Pour the mixture into a greased and floured cake tin and bake in

1 celery stalk, diced
1 leek, trimmed and sliced
1 carrot, peeled and sliced
150 g/5 oz butter
60 ml/2 fl oz brandy
½ bottle champagne or sparkling wine
3 egg yolks, beaten
200 ml/7 fl oz single cream

Boil the lobster in water with the bayleaf, salt and pepper, for about 15 minutes. Drain.

Peel the prawns and reserve the heads. Sauté the onion, celery, leek and carrot in 30 g/1 oz butter, then add the prawn heads. Flambé with the brandy, pour in the champagne or sparkling wine and simmer until reduced by half. Liquidize the sauce, pour into a saucepan and beat in the remaining butter and egg yolks over a very low heat. Add the prawns and heat through for 5 minutes. Remove from the heat and stir in the cream.

Preheat the oven to 220° C/425 ° F, gas mark 7. Split the lobster in half and arrange on a heatproof serving dish. Cover in sauce and brown in the oven for a few minutes.

CREAM JACKETS

Serves 6

6 large potatoes
100 g/3¹/₂ oz ham, diced
200 g/7 oz cooked, peeled prawns
parsley
salt and pepper
8 tbsp thick mayonnaise
60 ml/2 fl oz milk
100 ml/3¹/₂ fl oz double cream

Preheat the oven to 200° C/400° F, gas mark 6. Bake the potatoes in the oven for about 1 hour. Cut in half and scoop out the flesh, taking care not to break the skins. Raise the oven temperature to 230° C/450° F, gas mark 8. Mash the potato flesh and mix with the ham, parsley, salt, pepper, mayonnaise, milk and cream, and stuff the potato skins with this mixture. Return the stuffed potatoes to the oven for 5 minutes.

GYPSY EGGS

Serves 6

100 g/3¹/₂ oz butter
2 large onions, peeled and chopped
6 hard-boiled eggs, peeled
salt
¹/₄ tsp paprika

Opposite: Cream Jackets
Below: Gypsy Eggs

6 tomatoes, skinned, seeded and chopped
1 courgette, chopped
150 ml/5 fl oz cream
squeeze of lemon juice
3 tbsp dried breadcrumbs

Preheat the oven to 220° C/425° F, gas mark 7. Fry the onions in half the butter until soft. Cut the eggs in half and remove the yolks. Mix the yolks with half the onions, season with salt and paprika and use to stuff the egg whites. Arrange in an ovenproof dish, dot with the remaining butter and brown briefly in the oven. Add the tomatoes and courgette to the remaining onion in the frying-pan and cook for 5 minutes.

Spread the tomato and onion mixture in an ovenproof dish, then arrange the eggs on top. Mix the cream with the lemon juice and pour over. Sprinkle over the breadcrumbs and brown again.

COLD BUFFETS

PARTRIDGE AND HAZELNUT TERRINE

Serves 8

2 partridges
200 g/7 oz chicken livers
100 g/3½ oz streaky bacon, derinded and
roughly chopped
8 tbsp brandy
8 tbsp dry white wine
1 onion, peeled and quartered
2 carrots, peeled and halved
1 tsp thyme
1 bayleaf
black pepper
2 eggs, beaten
100 g/3½ oz hazelnuts, chopped

Place the partridges in a flameproof
casserole. Add the remaining ingredients,
except the eggs and hazelnuts, and just
enough water to cover. Bring to the boil,
cover and simmer for 1 hour.
   Preheat the oven to 180° C/350° F, gas
mark 4.
   Drain the partridges, reserving the
cooking liquid. Strain the cooking liquid
and retain both the liquid and the solid
ingredients. Remove and discard the skin
from the partridges and purée the flesh
with the reserved ingredients from the
cooking liquid. Add the beaten eggs and
chopped hazelnuts. If the mixture is too
thick, add some of the reserved cooking
liquid. Place the mixture in a mould and
cook in a bain-marie in the oven for about
30 minutes. When cold, cover with aspic,
if desired.

NORWEGIAN CAKE

Serves 6

4 gelatine leaves
3 eggs, separated
225 g/8 oz sugar
grated rind and juice of 1 orange
grated rind and juice of 1 lemon
225 ml/8 fl oz double or whipping cream
extra cream and orange segments

Soak the gelatine in 8 tablespoons cold
water. Meanwhile, beat together the egg
yolks with all but 2 tablespoons of the
sugar, until thick and creamy. Dissolve the

gelatine over low heat then stir into the
egg mixture with the grated rind and juice
of the orange and lemon. Set aside until
just beginning to thicken. Whip the 225
ml/8 fl oz cream, then fold into the egg
mixture. Beat the egg whites with the
remaining sugar and fold into the mixture.
Pour into a mould and refrigerate to set.
Decorate with extra whipped cream and
orange segments, if desired.

SMOKED SALMON TOAST

Serves 6

6 slices smoked salmon
6 eggs, beaten
6 slices bread, crusts removed
8 tbsp single cream
60 g/2 oz butter
salt

Toast the bread and reserve. Beat the eggs
with the cream and season with salt.
   Melt the butter in a saucepan, add the
eggs and cook over low heat, stirring.
Remove from the heat while still runny, as
they will continue to cook for a while.
   Arrange the toast on a dish and add
some scrambled eggs to each slice then
place a slice of smoked salmon on top.
Garnish with hard-boiled egg, lemon slices
and watercress, if desired.

AMERICAN LEG OF PORK

Serves 10

2 kg/4½ lb leg of pork, boned
2 litres/3½ pints white wine
2 carrots, roughly chopped
tarragon mustard
cloves
sugar
1 kg/2¼ lb canned pineapple chunks

Marinate the pork in the wine for 2 hours.
Place the pork and wine in a large pan,
add the carrots and enough cold water to
cover and bring to the boil. Lower the
heat and simmer for 1½ hours. Drain well
and place in a roasting tin.
   Preheat the oven to 180° C/350° F, gas
mark 4. Cut flaps in the top part of the
meat and put some mustard and a clove

under each flap. Pour on the liquid from
the canned cherries, the oil and some of
the pineapple juice from the can. Cover
loosely with foil and finish cooking in the
oven for 1 hour. Remove the pork from
the oven and place in another roasting tin.
Increase the oven temperature to 220°
C/425° F, gas mark 7. Cover the top of
the pork with the pineapple chunks and
cherries, sprinkle with sugar and brown in
the oven briefly.

HAM AND CHEESE TERRINE

Serves 8

5 eggs
150 ml/5 fl oz milk
60 g/2 oz butter
1 medium sliced bread loaf
6 slices ham
6 slices strong cheese

Preheat the oven to 180° C/350° F, gas
mark 4. Butter a terrine or eight individual
moulds and line with buttered greaseproof
paper. Beat together the eggs and milk,
melt the butter and combine with the
eggs. Cut the bread to fit the terrine or
moulds. Dip the bread in the egg mixture
then line the dish with it, putting a layer
of ham and cheese on top. Place the next
soaked slice on top and continue layering
until all the bread, ham and cheese is used
up. Pour on the remaining liquid and
cover with aluminium foil. Bake in the
oven for about 30 minutes, until the egg
sets. Remove, weigh down lightly and
leave to cool. Unmould and serve with a
sauce of melted Roquefort and butter, if
desired. Garnish with ham strips.

Top: Smoked Salmon Toast
Bottom: Ham and Cheese Terrine

PHEASANT PIE

Serves 6

For the filling:
1 pheasant with giblets, skinned
1/2 bottle white wine
1/4 tsp mixed herbs
60 g/2 oz smoked streaky bacon, derinded and diced
100 g/3 1/2 oz finely minced pork
1 truffle, finely chopped
salt
pepper
2 thick slices ham, weighing 150 g/5 oz each, diced
4 tbsp brandy
2 carrots, diced
1 onion, peeled and chopped

For the crust:
500 g/1 lb 2 oz flour
250 g/9 oz butter, softened
1 tbsp olive oil
200 ml/7 fl oz water
3 egg yolks
salt

Remove the pheasant meat from the bones. Place in a non-aluminium dish with the giblets and add just enough white wine to cover. Add the mixed herbs and leave to marinate for 24 hours, stirring occasionally.

Place the flour on a pastry board and make a well in the centre. Put the softened butter in the centre with the oil, 2 of the egg yolks, water and a pinch of salt. Mix together, knead until smooth then roll out and use three-quarters to line a buttered terrine or pie dish. Sprinkle over the diced bacon. Drain the pheasant and giblets and chop finely. Combine with half the minced pork, the chopped truffle, salt and pepper. Warm the diced ham in the brandy. Arrange successive layers of pheasant mixture, minced pork and ham in the terrine, finishing with a layer of the minced pork. Cover with the remaining dough, moistening the edges to join with the lining. Make a small air hole in the centre of the pie. Preheat the oven to 180° C/350° F, gas mark 4. Brush the top with the remaining egg yolk diluted in a little water. Bake in the oven for 2 1/2 hours. The dough should be golden, so increase the heat 15 minutes before the end of cooking time, if necessary.

Meanwhile, add the pheasant carcass, carrots and onion to the marinade. Simmer to reduce. Strain through muslin. Allow the cooked pie to cool a little, then pour the liquid through the hole in the top of the pie. Leave to cool.

This pie can be made either with one chicken or two partridges as an alternative to pheasant. If partridges are used, substitute red wine for white in the marinade.

MUSHROOM VOL-AU-VENTS

Serves 6

250 g/9 oz button mushrooms, sliced
250 ml/9 fl oz white wine
juice of 1 lemon
30 g/1 oz butter
250 ml/9 fl oz Béchamel sauce
100 g/3 1/2 oz Serrano ham or coppa, finely chopped
salt
grated nutmeg
12 cooked vol-au-vent cases

Preheat the oven to 220° C/425° F, gas mark 7. Place in a saucepan the mushrooms, white wine, lemon juice and butter and simmer for about 10 minutes. Drain, reserving the liquid. Mix together the Béchamel sauce, chopped ham, mushrooms and cooking liquid. Season with salt and grated nutmeg. Fill the vol-au-vent cases with this mixture, heat through for 5 minutes and serve piping hot.

SPANISH BEEF REDONDO

Serves 8

100 g/3 1/2 oz lard
1 kg/2 1/4 lb beef topside
100 g/3 1/2 oz streaky bacon, derinded and chopped
100 ml/3 1/2 fl oz beef stock
2 tomatoes, peeled and chopped
2 onions, peeled and chopped
2 leeks, cleaned and chopped
2 garlic cloves, chopped
1 clove
1 bayleaf
salt
pepper
60 ml/2 fl oz dry white wine or dry sherry

Preheat the oven to 180° C/350° F, gas mark 4. Heat the lard in a casserole, add the beef and bacon and brown the meat on all sides. Add the vegetables and garlic and sauté for 3 minutes. Add the stock, clove, bayleaf and salt and pepper. Cook in the oven for about 1 1/4 hours. Add the wine when the meat is almost done. Place the meat on a heated serving dish. Liquidize the sauce and serve separately in a sauceboat.

CHOCOLATE MOUSSE

Serves 6

100 g/3 1/2 oz milk chocolate
100 ml/3 1/2 fl oz strong coffee
3 tbsp brandy
100 g/3 1/2 oz castor sugar
2 eggs, separated
225 ml/8 fl oz double or whipping cream

Melt the chocolate in a bain-marie, then add the coffee, brandy and sugar, stirring constantly. Remove from the heat, allow to cool slightly and add the egg yolks. Beat the cream and fold in carefully. Beat the egg whites until stiff and fold in carefully. Divide the mousse among individual serving dishes and chill until ready to serve. Serve with langue de chat biscuits.

ALMOND AND FRUIT DELIGHT

Serves 5

250 g/9 oz sugar
250 ml/9 fl oz water
3 eggs
3 egg yolks
100 g/3 1/2 oz ground almonds
60 g/2 oz mixed, crystallized fruit, finely chopped

For decoration:
whipped cream
melted chocolate

Place all but 1 tablespoon of the sugar in a saucepan with the water, heat to dissolve the sugar then simmer for 10 minutes.

Preheat the oven to 180° C/350° F, gas mark 4.

Beat the eggs and egg yolks then add the almonds, syrup and chopped fruit. Take a shallow round or square cake tin and gently toast the remaining sugar in it on a very low heat, until the sugar becomes transparent. Pour the almond and fruit mixture on top. Place in a bain-marie and cook in the oven for 45 minutes or until a skewer inserted into the centre comes out clean. Allow to cool, turn out on to a glass dish and decorate with melted chocolate and whipped cream.

Top: Chocolate Mousse
Bottom: Almond and Fruit Delight

COLD ROAST BEEF

Serves 8

2 tbsp lard
2 tbsp oil
salt
pepper
2 kg/4½ lb beef fillet

Ask your butcher to tie the meat so that it will retain its shape during cooking.

Preheat the oven to 240° C/475° F, gas mark 9. Heat the lard and oil in a roasting tin until very hot. Season the beef then place in the tin and roast in the oven for 20 minutes, turning and basting occasionally with the fats and juices. The meat is ready when it is still very pink inside. Allow to cool completely before slicing thinly. Serve with a selection of salads.

HAM WITH RASPBERRY SAUCE

Serves 4

4 x 120 g/4 oz slices ham
pepper
45 g/1½ oz butter
1 tbsp cornflour
100 ml/3½ fl oz chicken or beef stock, cold
salt
60 ml/2 fl oz cherry liqueur
150 g/5 oz demerara sugar
1 tbsp mustard
1 tsp mixed herbs
1 medium jar raspberry jam
juice of 1 orange
juice of 1 lemon
8 tbsp port
8 tbsp single cream

Season the ham with the pepper. Melt the butter in a frying-pan, add the cornflour and cold stock and mix into a smooth paste. Add the cherry liqueur, sugar, mustard and a pinch of mixed herbs. Sauté the ham in this sauce for about 10 minutes.

For the raspberry sauce, mix together the jam, lemon and orange juices, port, salt and pepper and heat through. Remove from the heat and add the cream.

RICE WITH PRAWNS AND MAYONNAISE

Serves 4

300 g/10 oz prawns in shells
1 onion, peeled and finely chopped
4 garlic cloves, finely chopped
4 tbsp oil
2 tbsp finely chopped parsley
100 ml/3½ fl oz fresh tomato sauce
200 g/7 oz rice
150 g/5 oz cooked peas
salt
pinch of curry powder

Peel the prawns and, using the heads and shells, make a stock which is twice the volume of the rice. Reserve.

Sauté the onion and garlic in the oil until soft. Add the parsley, tomato sauce and rice, stir, and add the prawns, peas, reserved prawn stock, salt and curry powder. Simmer for 20 minutes or until the rice is cooked. Serve with a bowl of mayonnaise on the side.

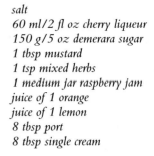

**Top: Ham with Raspberry Sauce
Bottom: Rice with Prawns and Mayonnaise**

SPONTANEOUS ENTERTAINING

GYPSY CHOPS

Serves 4

4 veal chops
2 tbsp oil
500 g/1 lb 2 oz tomatoes, peeled and chopped
2 peppers, halved and seeded
salt & pepper
75 g/2¹/₂ oz cucumber, finely chopped
60 g/2 oz black olives, chopped
2 hard-boiled eggs, shelled and sliced

Brown the chops in the oil in a frying-pan. Cut the peppers into strips, add to the pan with the tomatoes and cook for 20 minutes. A few minutes before the end of cooking time, season and add the chopped cucumber and olives. Arrange the vegetables in a serving dish, place the chops on top and garnish with sliced hard-boiled eggs.

VEAL CHOPS WITH HAZELNUT SAUCE

Serves 6

6 veal chops
3 tbsp flour
oil for frying
salt & pepper
500 g/1 lb 2 oz onions, peeled and chopped
2 garlic cloves, chopped
6 tbsp fresh tomato sauce
100 ml/3¹/₂ fl oz white wine
150 g/5 oz ground hazelnuts
10 tbsp single cream

For the garnish:
6 small eating apples

Dust the chops with the flour and brown in very hot oil. Remove and reserve. Add the chopped onions and garlic to the pan, with the tomato sauce, wine and enough water or stock to moisten. Simmer for 10 minutes. Purée the onion mixture and put into a flameproof casserole. Stir in the hazelnuts and add the chops. Season, cover and cook for about 15 minutes, until the meat is tender. Remove the chops and stir in the cream off the heat.

To prepare the apples, core them and place in a baking dish with a little water, brandy and butter. Bake in the oven for about 20 minutes, depending on the type of apple used.

Arrange the chops on a serving dish, pour over the sauce and garnish with the apples.

Top: Gypsy Chops
Bottom: Veal Chops with Hazelnut Sauce

ASPARAGUS AU GRATIN

Serves 5

1.25 kg/2³/₄ lb asparagus, trimmed
60 g/2 oz butter
45 g/1¹/₂ oz flour
1 litre/1³/₄ pints milk, warmed
salt
nutmeg
150 g/5 oz cheese, grated
3 eggs, separated

Simmer the asparagus upright in a large pan of salted water for about 10 minutes, until tender. Drain carefully, making sure the tips do not break. Make a Béchamel sauce; melt the butter, add the flour and stir in the warm milk, a little at a time. Season with salt and a pinch of nutmeg. Simmer for about 10 minutes, stirring constantly until smooth and creamy.

Meanwhile, preheat the oven to 180° C/350° F, gas mark 4.

Remove the Béchamel sauce from the heat and add the cheese and egg yolks. Beat the egg whites until stiff and carefully fold in. Place the asparagus in an ovenproof dish, pour over the sauce and heat in the oven for 20 minutes. Finish by sprinkling with a little extra cheese and browning briefly under the grill.

GARLIC PRAWNS

Serves 4

75 ml/2½ fl oz oil
5 garlic cloves, chopped
2 chilis, seeds removed, roughly chopped

1 tbsp chopped parsley
500 g/1 lb 2 oz peeled prawns
salt

Heat the oil in a large frying-pan, add the chopped garlic and cook for 1 minute. Then add the chopped chilis and parsley and finally the peeled prawns and salt to taste. Fry for a few minutes then serve in an earthenware dish. Add a little paprika if you want the dish to be more spicy.

Opposite: Asparagus au Gratin
Below: Garlic Prawns

CHEESE SOUFFLÉ

Serves 4

60 g/2 oz butter
2 heaped tbsp flour
250 ml/9 fl oz milk, warmed
salt & pepper
100 g/3½ oz Gruyère, grated
5 eggs, separated

Preheat the oven to 180° C/350° F, gas mark 4. Make a Béchamel sauce; melt half the butter, stir in the flour and then the milk. Simmer for 10 minutes, season with salt and pepper and add the cheese, stirring constantly. Remove from the heat, allow to cool slightly, then add the egg yolks. Beat the whites to form stiff peaks and fold into the sauce carefully.

Use the remaining butter to grease a soufflé dish. Pour in the mixture. It should not come right up to the top, as the soufflé will rise. Cook in the oven for 10 minutes, then increase the heat to 220° C/425° F, gas mark 7 and cook for a further 10 minutes.

PUREED POTATO MOUSSELINE

Serves 4

250 g/9 oz potatoes, peeled
100 ml/3½ fl oz milk
100 g/3½ oz butter
8 tbsp single cream
salt
nutmeg
200 g/7 oz ham, cut into strips

Place the potatoes in cold, salted water, bring to the boil, cover and cook for 20 minutes. Drain and purée the potatoes, adding the hot milk and butter. Finally, add the cream, salt and nutmeg.

To serve, line a shallow ovenproof dish with the potato purée, sprinkle over the ham, cover with another layer of potato, add another layer of ham and continue layering, finishing with the ham.

GOLDEN ORANGES

Serves 6

6 oranges
45 g/1½ oz butter
60 ml/2 fl oz Grand Marnier
1 tbsp cornflour
250 ml/9 fl oz clear syrup
150 ml/5 fl oz yoghurt

Preheat the oven to 180° C/350° F, gas mark 4. Peel the oranges and slice them. Cut the peel from one of the oranges into matchstick shreds. Arrange the orange slices in an ovenproof dish. Melt the butter, add the Grand Marnier, cornflour and syrup and pour over the oranges. Bake in the oven for 15 minutes. Meanwhile, blanch the shredded peel. Drain the oranges, then beat the yoghurt and orange shreds into the sauce. Pour the sauce over the oranges and serve at room temperature.

PASTA SHELLS WITH MOZZARELLA

Serves 4

200 g/7 oz pasta shells
60 g/2 oz butter
salt
pepper
100 g/3½ oz ham, shredded
150 g/5 oz Mozzarella cheese, grated
8 tbsp milk
100 ml/ 3½ fl oz single cream
¼ tsp nutmeg
2 hard-boiled eggs, shelled and chopped
1 tbsp chopped parsley

Boil the pasta in plenty of salted water for 10-15 minutes. Drain and add a little of the butter. Melt the remaining butter and add the ham, cheese, milk, cream, nutmeg and salt. Mix this into the pasta. Serve very hot, garnished with chopped, hard-boiled eggs and parsley.

HAITI BANANAS

Serves 6

8 bananas
75 g/2½ oz butter
100 g/3½ oz sugar
juice of 2 lemons
100 ml/3½ fl oz rum
60 g/2 oz desiccated coconut

Peel the bananas and leave them whole. Melt the butter in a frying-pan and brown the bananas. Remove to a serving dish. Add the sugar, lemon juice and rum to the pan and cook for 10 minutes. Pour over the bananas, sprinkle with coconut and serve.

SCRAMBLED EGGS WITH PRAWNS AND CHEESE

Serves 4

75 g/ 2½ oz butter
300 g/10 oz prawns, peeled
150 g/5 oz Emmenthal cheese, diced
8 eggs, beaten
salt
pepper
1 tbsp chopped parsley
8 tbsp single cream

Melt the butter in a mixing bowl over a pan of simmering water. Add the prawns and cheese. Season the eggs with salt, pepper and chopped parsley and pour over the prawns. Continue to cook, stirring constantly, for about 5 minutes until it thickens. Remove from the heat, add the cream and serve immediately.

ANDALUSIAN EGGS

Serves 4

250 ml/9 fl oz fresh tomato sauce
100 g/3½ oz ham, diced
100 g/3½ oz chorizo, diced
75 g/2½ oz cooked peas
100 g/3½ oz potato, peeled, cubed and fried
2 canned pimientos, cut into strips
8 eggs

Preheat the oven to 180° C/350° F, gas mark 4. Divide the tomato sauce between 4 individual ovenproof dishes. Add the ham, chorizo, cooked peas, fried potato and pimientos. Make a space in the middle and break 2 eggs into it. Bake in the oven for about 5 minutes, until the egg whites are set but the yolks still runny. Serve at once.

Top: Scrambled Eggs with Prawns and Cheese
Bottom: Andalusian Eggs

DINNER PARTIES

FLEMISH BEEF STEW

Serves 4

550 g/1¹/₄ lb stewing steak, cubed
salt
black pepper
60 ml/2 fl oz oil
250 g/9 oz onions, peeled and finely chopped

4 garlic cloves, finely chopped
150 g/5 oz bacon, derinded and chopped
1 tbsp flour
225 ml/8 fl oz stout
225 ml/8 fl oz beef stock
1 tsp chopped thyme
1 bayleaf
2 tsp vinegar
1 tbsp chopped parsley

Season the meat with salt and pepper. Heat the oil in a flameproof casserole and brown the meat over a high heat. Remove and reserve. Add the onions and garlic to the casserole and sauté for 5 minutes. Stir in the bacon and flour, and as soon as the bacon begins to colour, add the beer, stock, reserved meat, thyme, bayleaf and vinegar. Cover and cook on a low heat for 1¹/₄ hours until the beef is just done. Sprinkle with parsley and serve with boiled white rice.

LAYERED BEEF CASSEROLE

Serves 4

550 g/1¹/₄ lb beef fillet, cubed
salt
pepper
2 tbsp oil
500 g/1 lb 2 oz potatoes, peeled and sliced finely
¹/₂ tsp oregano
¹/₂ tsp thyme
2 onions, peeled and sliced
500 g/1 lb 2 oz tomatoes, skinned, seeded and chopped
8 tbsp white wine

Season the meat with salt and pepper. Put a little oil in a flameproof casserole, then arrange half the potatoes in a layer, sprinkle on a little oregano and thyme then arrange the onions on top. Add the meat and chopped tomatoes. Finish with a layer of the remaining potatoes. Pour over the wine and sprinkle on more oregano and thyme. Cover and cook slowly for about 40 minutes. Serve very hot.

CHICKEN LIVER AND TRUFFLE PATE

Serves 6

550 g/1¹/₄ lb chicken livers
100 g/3¹/₂ oz butter
8 tbsp brandy
4 tbsp white wine

Left, top: Flemish Beef Stew
Left, bottom: Layered Beef Casserole
Opposite, top: Chicken Liver and Truffle Pâté
Opposite, bottom: Mixed Fish Stew

4 tbsp chicken or beef stock
1 small can truffles, thinly sliced, liquid reserved
salt
black pepper
100 g/3¹/₂ oz ham

Clean and chop the livers. Place in a frying-pan with the butter, brandy, wine, stock, truffle liquid, salt and pepper and simmer for 20 minutes, stirring occasionally. Purée the livers in a blender or food processor and stir in the chopped ham and truffle slices. Turn into 6 individual dishes or one large dish and chill until they set, about 4 hours.

MIXED FISH STEW

Serves 8

1 kg/2¹/₄ lb mussels
400 g/14 oz cooked prawns, peeled, shells reserved

6 cooked Dublin Bay prawns, peeled, shells reserved
120-170 g/4-6 oz flour
500 g/1 lb 2 oz monkfish, cubed
500 g/1 lb 2 oz sea bass or other firm white fish, cubed
500 g/1 lb 2 oz squid, cut in rings
120 ml/4 fl oz oil
1 large onion, peeled and finely chopped
3 garlic cloves, finely chopped
60 ml/2 fl oz brandy
250 ml/9 fl oz fresh tomato sauce
250 ml/9 fl oz white wine
1 tbsp chopped parsley

salt
pepper

Rinse the mussels thoroughly in cold water, discarding any which do not shut immediately when sharply tapped. Steam open in a little salted water, discarding any which do not open. Set aside and reserve the mussels in half-shells to which they are attached. Discard the empty half-shells. Strain the cooking liquid into a saucepan, add the prawn shells and simmer to reduce by half. Strain the liquid and reserve, discarding the prawn shells. Dredge in

flour the pieces of monkfish, sea bass and squid. Sauté in hot oil for 5 minutes, then transfer to a flameproof casserole.

Sauté the onions and garlic in a little oil, add the brandy and flambé, then add the tomato sauce, white wine, prawn shell stock and some chopped parsley. Season with salt and pepper and pour over the fish. Add the prawns and cook gently for 10 minutes. Serve in the casserole garnished with the mussels.

RICE SALAD

Serves 4

200 g/7 oz white rice
salt
1 cooked chicken breast

2 pimientos, finely sliced
150 g/5 oz stoned green olives, chopped
250 g/9 oz tomatoes, skinned, seeded and chopped
1 can anchovies, chopped
1 onion, peeled and finely chopped
85 ml/3 fl oz olive oil
30 ml/1 fl oz tarragon vinegar
1 small can asparagus tips

Cook the rice in plenty of boiling, salted water for 20 minutes. Drain, refresh and

cool. Remove and discard the chicken skin and bone, and cut the flesh into chunks. Mix together the cold rice with the pimientos, olives, tomatoes, anchovies and chopped onion. Season with oil, vinegar and salt and place on a serving dish. Arrange the chicken pieces and asparagus tips on top.

MARINARA CLAMS

Serves 6

1 kg/2¹/₄ lb clams
100 ml/3¹/₂ fl oz oil
1 onion, peeled and finely chopped
2 garlic cloves, chopped
2 tsp fresh breadcrumbs
100 ml/3
¹/₂ fl oz white wine
1 bayleaf
juice of 1 lemon
2 tbsp chopped parsley
salt
pepper

Opposite: Rice Salad
Below: Marinara Clams

Rinse the clams thoroughly, discarding any which do not open immediately when sharply tapped. Place in a frying-pan with a little cold water. Heat until the shells open, discarding any that remain closed, then strain the cooking juices through muslin and reserve. Heat the oil in a flameproof casserole and sauté the chopped onion and garlic. Add the breadcrumbs and stir, then add the strained clam juice, wine, bayleaf, lemon juice, half the parsley, and the salt and pepper. Add the clams and simmer together for 10 minutes. Serve sprinkled with the remaining parsley.

HAM AND ASPARAGUS SALAD

Serves 6

300 g/10 oz carrots, peeled and chopped
300 g/10 oz French beans, peeled and chopped
250 g/9 oz shelled peas
500 ml/18 fl oz mayonnaise
6 slices ham
1 kg/2¼ lb canned asparagus
250 g/9 oz stoned black olives
3 hard-boiled eggs, sliced

**Top: Ham and Asparagus Salad
Bottom: Liver in Sherry Sauce**

Simmer together the carrots, French beans and peas until just tender. Drain and cool, then mix in enough of the mayonnaise to bind. Use the mixture to fill the slices of ham and roll up. Arrange the rolls on a serving dish and garnish with the asparagus, olives and slices of hard-boiled egg. Serve the remaining mayonnaise separately.

COLD FILLET OF BEEF

Serves 7

For the beef:
1 kg/2¼ lb beef fillet
salt
pepper
100 g/3½ oz streaky bacon
4 tbsp oil
100 g/3½ oz lard
3 garlic cloves
8 tbsp white wine

For the Russian salad:
100 g/3½ oz potatoes, peeled and diced
300 g/10 oz carrots, peeled and diced
250 g/9 oz shelled peas
150 g/5 oz French beans, diced
500 ml/18 fl oz mayonnaise

Preheat the oven to 220° C/425° F, gas mark 7. Rub the beef with salt and pepper, then wrap with the bacon, securing with string. Heat the oil and lard in a roasting tin, brown the garlic and put in the meat. Roast in the oven for 45 minutes, basting frequently with the fat and juices, and adding the wine half way through. Allow to cool.

For the Russian salad, cook all the vegetables in boiling, salted water. Drain and cool, then mix in the mayonnaise.

Slice the cold meat and arrange on a serving dish with the salad in a mound in the centre.

LIVER IN SHERRY SAUCE

Serves 4

500 g/1 lb 2 oz lambs' liver
salt
pepper
120 ml/4 fl oz oil
60 g/2 oz flour
1 onion, peeled and finely chopped
100 g/3½ oz bacon, derinded and chopped
100 ml/3½ fl oz dry sherry
100 ml/3½ fl oz chicken stock
500 g/18 oz potatoes, peeled and boiled
250 g/9 oz carrots, peeled and boiled

Slice the liver into small pieces, season with salt and pepper, and sauté in half the oil for 5 minutes. Add the remaining oil to the pan and fry the onion and bacon together, then stir in the flour and cook until it begins to colour. Add the sherry and stock and simmer for 15 minutes. Add the liver to the sauce, season with pepper and cook for a further 15 minutes. Serve very hot, accompanied by the boiled potatoes and carrots.

PRAWN AND WALNUT COCKTAIL

Serves 4

100 g/3½ oz walnut halves
1 tsp brandy
1 tsp mustard
1 tsp tomato ketchup
salt
pepper
250 ml/9 fl oz mayonnaise
500 g/1 lb 2 oz cooked, peeled prawns
1 cucumber, finely sliced
1 celery stalk, finely diced
1 lettuce

Reserve a few walnuts for the garnish and chop the remainder.

Add the brandy, mustard, tomato ketchup, salt and pepper to the mayonnaise. Mix together with the prawns, walnuts, cucumber and celery.

Wash, dry and cut the lettuce into strips, and use to line 4 cocktail glasses. Heap the prawn cocktail on to the lettuce and garnish with walnuts.

SPICY BUTTON MUSHROOMS

Serves 4

60 g/2 oz butter
250 g/9 oz button mushrooms, quartered
5 garlic cloves, finely chopped
100 ml/3½ fl oz chicken stock
4 tbsp fresh tomato sauce
juice of ½ lemon
1 bayleaf
1-2 tsp chili powder
salt
1 tbsp flour

Melt the butter in a frying-pan and add the mushrooms, garlic, stock, tomato sauce, lemon juice, bayleaf and chili powder. Season with salt.

Cook over a low heat for 20 minutes. If the sauce is too thin, mix some of the pan juices with the flour, then return it to the pan, stirring, and cook for another 2 minutes.

Serve hot or cold.

SPRING PEARS

Serves 6

6 pears, peeled and halved lengthways
250 ml/9 fl oz sugar
8 tbsp single cream
100 g/3½ oz Philadelphia cheese
100 g/3½ oz walnuts, chopped
6 tbsp strawberry or raspberry jam
75 g/2½ oz sugar

Place the pear halves in a large pan, pour over the syrup, bring to the boil then simmer for 20 minutes until soft. Remove the pears and allow to cool. Simmer the syrup until very thick.

Thoroughly mix together the cream, cheese, chopped walnuts, jam and sugar. Spread the mixture on a round serving dish, arrange the pears, cut side down in a circle on top and pour over the cold syrup.

**Top: Prawn and Walnut Cocktail
Bottom: Spicy Button Mushrooms**

LUNCH AND SUPPER DISHES

HAM AND PEACHES

Serves 4

500 g/1 lb 2 oz canned peaches in syrup
4 x 100 g/3¹/₂ oz slices ham
pepper
60 g/2 oz butter
1 tbsp cornflour
juice of 1 orange
juice of 1 lemon
100 g/3¹/₂ oz cooked prunes

Drain the peaches, reserving 100 ml/3¹/₂ fl oz of syrup. Season the ham with pepper. Melt the butter and add the peach syrup. Mix the cornflour with the orange and lemon juice and add to the pan. Cook until slightly thickened, then add the ham and simmer for 10 minutes. Place the ham on a serving dish, pour over the sauce and garnish with the peaches and prunes.

PUFF PASTRIES WITH BUTTON MUSHROOMS

Serves 8

200 g/7 oz button mushrooms, sliced
60 ml/2 fl oz white wine
250 ml/9 fl oz warm Béchamel sauce
salt
pepper
¹/₂ tsp nutmeg
60 g/2 oz butter
1 egg yolk
18 small vol-au-vent cases

Simmer the mushrooms in the wine until tender, drain and add to the Béchamel sauce. Season with salt, pepper and nutmeg. Heat to boiling point, then remove from the heat and add the butter and egg yolk. Stir until a creamy sauce is achieved. Meanwhile, warm the vol-au-vent cases in the oven, then fill with the mushroom sauce. If the sauce needs to be reheated, heat over a pan of boiling water to prevent curdling.

MULTICOLOURED SALAD

Serves 6

250 g/9 oz Edam or Gouda, cubed
2 hard-boiled eggs, peeled and quartered
100 g/3¹/₂ oz ham
500 g/1 lb 2 oz tomatoes, sliced
200 g/7 oz button mushrooms, sliced and cooked
250 ml/9 fl oz mayonnaise or vinaigrette
2 apples
2 tsp lemon juice

Peel, core and slice the apples. Sprinkle with the lemon juice to prevent discoloration.

Arrange all the ingredients, except the mayonnaise or vinaigrette if using, on a round or oval serving dish. Serve the mayonnaise or vinaigrette separately. Alternatively, serve the salad on a bed of shredded lettuce in a salad bowl.

TUNA VOL-AU-VENTS

Serves 3-6

6 small vol-au-vent cases
¹/₂ onion, peeled and finely chopped
2 tbsp oil
250 g/9 oz canned pimientos, finely chopped
250 ml/9 fl oz fresh tomato sauce
salt and pepper

Preheat the oven to 170° C/325° F, gas mark 3. Warm the vol-au-vent cases in the oven. Meanwhile, sauté the onion in the oil until pale golden. Separate the tuna into flakes and add to the onion with the pimientos and tomato sauce. Season and use to fill the warmed vol-au-vents.

GAZPACHO

Serves 4

150 g/5 oz breadcrumbs
250 g/9 oz tomatoes, roughly chopped
1 green pepper, seeded and chopped
1 garlic clove, chopped
salt
5 tbsp oil
2 tbsp wine vinegar
1 litre/1³/₄ pints water

Soak the breadcrumbs in a little cold water then place in a blender or food processor with the tomatoes, pepper, garlic and salt. Liquidize, adding the oil slowly, as though making mayonnaise. When all the oil is absorbed, add the vinegar and cold water. Sieve the mixture and refrigerate. Serve with diced tomato, cucumber and bread on the side.

HAM MOUSSE

Serves 6

100 ml/3¹/₂ fl oz chicken stock
8 tbsp rum
1 bayleaf
salt
pepper
200 g/7 oz York ham, finely chopped
200 g/7 oz cooked ham, finely chopped
2 eggs, separated
8 tbsp double cream
4 tbsp liquid gelatine

Place the stock in a saucepan and add the rum, bayleaf, salt and pepper. Add both types of ham, bring to the boil and simmer for 12 minutes. Liquidize the contents of the pan and pour into a mixing bowl. Stir in the egg yolks and cream. Beat the egg whites until stiff then fold in with the warm gelatine, taste and adjust the seasoning. Pour into a mould and chill for at least 3 hours.

PRAWN AND HAKE RAMEKINS

Serves 6

6 tbsp oil
1 onion, peeled and finely chopped
1 garlic clove, finely chopped
100 ml/3¹/₂ fl oz fresh tomato sauce
500 g/1 .b 2 oz cooked, peeled prawns
500 g/1 lb 2 oz hake, skinned and diced
4 tbsp dry sherry
100 g/3¹/₂ oz canned tuna, flaked
4 eggs, beaten
salt
pepper
parsley sprigs

Top: Multicoloured Salad
Bottom: Ham Mousse

Heat the oil in a large pan and sauté the chopped onion and garlic for a few minutes. Add the tomato sauce, prawns, diced hake, sherry and tuna. Cover and simmer for about 15 minutes, until the hake is tender.

Preheat the oven to 180° C/350° F, gas mark 4. Remove from the heat and add the beaten eggs, and season with salt and pepper, stirring well. Butter 6 individual ramekins and pour in the mixture. Place in a bain–marie and cook in the oven for 30 minutes, until set.

Serve hot, accompanied by a tomato sauce or Béchamel sauce, or allow to cool in the ramekins then turn out and serve cold with a mayonnaise, garnished with parsley sprigs, extra prawns and sliced hard–boiled eggs.

PATE AND WILD MUSHROOMS ON TOAST

Serves 6

90 g/3 oz butter
12 wild, flat cap or oyster mushrooms, thickly sliced
salt
1 tsp wine or sherry vinegar
3 slices bacon, halved
6 slices bread
90 g/3 oz smooth meat pâté

Melt just over half the butter in a frying-pan, add the mushrooms and cook on a high heat for 4 minutes. Season with salt and vinegar. Grill the bacon on both sides. Toast the bread and spread with the remaining butter and the pâté. Arrange the bacon and mushrooms on top and serve immediately.

PRAWNS IN AVOCADO WITH PINK SAUCE

Serves 8

500 g/1 lb 2 oz cooked, peeled prawns
2 tbsp fresh tomato sauce
2 tbsp tomato ketchup
2 tbsp brandy
500 ml/18 fl oz mayonnaise
4 avocados
salt
2 tbsp chopped parsley
½ lettuce, finely shredded

Chop the prawns finely, reserving a few

for garnish. Add the tomato sauce, tomato ketchup and brandy to the mayonnaise. Halve the avocados, remove the flesh from the skin and mix together with the prawns and mayonnaise. Season with salt and refill the skins. Garnish with the remaining prawns and sprinkle with chopped parsley.

Serve on a bed of finely shredded lettuce.

TAPENADE TOAST

Serves 6

12 thick slices of bread
24 stoned black olives
3 anchovy fillets
2 tbsp capers
olive oil as required
pepper

Opposite: Prawn and Hake Ramekins
Below: Prawns in Avocado with Pink Sauce

Preheat the oven to 170° C/325° F, gas mark 3. Warm the bread slices in the oven without allowing them to brown. Meanwhile, prepare the tapenade. Place the olives in a mortar with the anchovy fillets and capers, and pound them together, gradually adding enough olive oil to make a rough paste of spreading consistency. Season with pepper and spread the warmed bread with the paste

The tapenade can be made by mixing all the ingredients in a food processor or blender to save time.

FIRST COURSES

FISH IN ROMESCU SAUCE

Serves 8

*1 kg/2¹/₄ lb uncooked Dublin Bay or king
prawns
200 ml/7 fl oz olive oil
salt & pepper
1 tbsp chopped parsley
1 kg/2¹/₄ lb mussels
6 boneless monkfish fillets, cubed
500 g/1 lb 2 oz squid, sliced into rings
flour for dredging
oil for frying
5 garlic cloves, chopped
100 g/3¹/₂ oz hazelnuts, chopped
¹/₂ tsp chili powder
250 ml/9 fl oz white wine*

Marinate the prawns in the olive oil, salt
and parsley for 2 hours. Rinse the mussels
thoroughly in cold water, discarding any
that do not shut when sharply tapped.
Steam the mussels in a little water, strain
and reserve the cooking liquid. Discard
any mussels that have not opened.
Remove the mussels from their shells and
place in a flameproof casserole. Dredge the
monkfish and squid rings in flour and fry
in oil for 5 minutes. Cook the prawns on a
griddle or in a frying-pan, peel and add to
the mussels in the casserole. Fry the garlic
cloves then pound together with the
hazelnuts, chili powder, and salt and
pepper. Add the wine and reserved mussel
cooking liquid. Pour into the casserole and
simmer for 10 minutes. Serve straight from
the casserole. This dish tastes even better
the following day.

SPAGHETTI NAPOLITANA

Serves 5

*1 onion, peeled and finely chopped
2 garlic cloves, finely chopped
200 g/7 oz button mushrooms, sliced
150 g/5 oz ham
2 tbsp olive oil
¹/₂ tsp oregano
salt
pepper
8 tbsp fresh tomato sauce
225 ml/8 fl oz chicken stock
250 g/9 oz spaghetti
15 g/¹/₂ oz butter
100 g/3¹/₂ oz grated Parmesan cheese*

Sauté the chopped onion, garlic,
mushrooms and ham in the olive oil. Add
the tomato sauce, stock, oregano, salt and
pepper. Cover and simmer for about 20
minutes. Meanwhile, cook the spaghetti
in plenty of boiling, salted water and add
the butter. Stir the hot sauce into the pasta
and serve with grated Parmesan cheese.

ARANJUEZ EGGS

Serves 6

*250 g/9 oz fresh asparagus
salt
60 g/2 oz butter
1 tbsp flour
3 egg yolks
150 ml/5 fl oz single cream
6 poached eggs
6 slices ham
1 hard-boiled egg, shelled and chopped
1 truffle, chopped*

Simmer the asparagus in boiling, salted
water until tender. Drain, reserving the
cooking liquid, and purée half the
asparagus, reserving the tips. Melt the
butter in a saucepan, stir in the flour, cook
briefly then add the reserved cooking
liquid. Simmer for 5 minutes then stir in
the puréed asparagus, egg yolks and cream.
Season with salt and reserve.
   Place a poached egg and a few asparagus
tips on each slice of ham, roll up and
arrange in a large serving dish. Pour over
the sauce and garnish with the remaining
asparagus tips. Garnish with the chopped
hard-boiled egg and truffle and serve.

SPINACH SOUFFLE

Serves 6

*500 g/1 lb 2 oz spinach
90 g/3 oz butter
1 tbsp flour
salt
pepper
8 tbsp chicken stock
100 g/3¹/₂ oz ham, diced
60 g/2 oz grated cheese
3 egg yolks
4 egg whites*

Cook the spinach, drain well and chop
finely. Melt 30 g/1 oz of the butter in a
saucepan, add the spinach and cook briefly
on a high heat. Stir in the flour, and season
with salt and pepper. Add the stock and
simmer for 10 minutes. Remove from the
heat and add the diced ham, cheese, egg
yolks and half the remaining butter. Beat
the egg whites until stiff and fold in.
Grease a soufflé dish or 6 individual dishes
with the remaining butter and pour in the
mixture. Cook in the oven for 25 minutes
and serve immediately.

KING PRAWNS WITH
TARTARE SAUCE

Serves 6

*1 kg/2¹/₄ lb uncooked king prawns
1 onion, peeled and finely sliced
sprig parsley
2 tbsp vinegar
salt
pepper
¹/₂ lettuce, finely shredded*

*For the tartare sauce:
250 ml/9 fl oz mayonnaise
2 hard-boiled eggs, shelled and finely chopped
1 tbsp chopped parsley
30 g/1 oz capers, chopped
30 g/2 oz gherkins, chopped
1 tbsp wine vinegar
salt
pepper*

Place the prawns in a frying-pan, cover
with cold water, add the sliced onion,
parsley, vinegar, salt and pepper. Bring to
the boil then remove from the heat.
Drain, place in iced water and reserve.
   For the tartare sauce, combine the
mayonnaise with the chopped eggs,
parsley, capers, gherkins and vinegar, mix
well and season with salt and pepper.
   Drain the prawns and serve on a bed of
shredded lettuce with the tartare sauce.

**Top: King Prawns with Tartare Sauce
Bottom: Spinach Soufflé**

QUICHE LORRAINE

Serves 6

For the pastry:
200 g/7 oz flour
100 g/3½ oz butter, diced
4 tbsp water
½ tsp salt

For the filling:
5 eggs
12 tbsp milk
salt
pepper
100 g/3½ oz ham, diced
100 g/3½ oz Gruyère cheese, diced

For the pastry, place the flour on a board. Make a well in the centre, add the remaining ingredients and work with your fingers to achieve a smooth dough. Leave to stand for a few minutes in a cool place.

Meanwhile, preheat the oven to 180° C/350° F, gas mark 4. Roll out the pastry and use to line a flan tin. Prick the base all over then place in the oven for 15 minutes.

For the filling, beat the eggs with the milk and season with salt and pepper. When the pastry is ready, remove from the oven, sprinkle on the diced ham and cheese and pour in the egg mixture. Return to the oven for 15-20 minutes until set.

TUNA AND OLIVE TIMBALE

Serves 4

90 ml/3 fl oz milk
8 eggs
¼ tsp nutmeg
salt
200 g/7 oz canned tuna in oil, drained and mashed
60 g/2 oz olives, chopped

1 pimiento, chopped
1 tbsp parsley
30 g/1 oz butter
250 ml/9 fl oz mayonnaise

Preheat the oven to 180° C/350° F, gas mark 4. Warm the milk. Beat the eggs and add the warmed milk and nutmeg and season with salt. Add the tuna, olives, pimiento and parsley. Butter an ovenproof dish or 4 individual timbales, pour in the mixture and place in a bain-marie. Cook in the oven for 35 minutes, until set. Turn out when cold and serve with mayonnaise. Garnish with extra olives, pimiento and parsley, if liked.

CREAM OF ASPARAGUS SOUP

Serves 4

60 g/2 oz butter
3 leeks, chopped
1 onion, peeled and chopped
1 medium can asparagus, drained, liquid reserved
225 ml/8 fl oz stock
6 tbsp single cream
salt
pepper
2 tsp chopped parsley

Melt the butter in a saucepan and add the chopped leeks, onion and all but the tips of the asparagus. Cook gently, then add the liquid from the asparagus can and the stock, simmer for a further 5 minutes. Liquidize, then add the cream, and season with salt and pepper. Reheat and add the asparagus tips and chopped parsley.

**Opposite: Tuna and Olive Timbale
Below: Cod Casserole (recipe on page 13)**

MAIN COURSES

HAKE AND COCKLES

Serves 6

6 hake or cod steaks
salt
pepper
3 tbsp flour
2 eggs, beaten
oil for frying
1 onion, peeled and finely chopped
1 garlic clove, finely chopped
200 g/7 oz canned cockles, drained, liquid reserved
8 tbsp white wine

Season the hake with salt and pepper, dust with 2 tbsp flour, coat with beaten egg and fry in hot oil. Drain thoroughly and arrange in an ovenproof dish.

Preheat the oven to 170° C/325° F, gas mark 3. Heat some more oil in the pan, add the chopped onion and garlic and fry for 2 minutes. Stir in the remaining flour and cook until lightly coloured. Add the reserved liquid from the canned cockles, the wine and enough water to make a smooth pouring sauce. Simmer for 2 minutes then strain and pour over the hake. Add the cockles and heat through in the oven for 10 minutes. Serve straight from the dish, garnished with lemon slices and finely chopped parsley, if desired.

ENTRECOTE CHASSEUR

Serves 4

120 g/4 oz butter
1 tbsp oil
4 entrecôte steaks
2 tbsp flour
250 g/9 oz onions, peeled and finely chopped
3 garlic cloves, finely chopped
60 ml/2 fl oz red wine
100 ml/3$^{1/2}$ fl oz beef stock
1 bayleaf
$^{1/2}$ tsp basil
1 tbsp chopped parsley
salt
250 g/9 oz button mushrooms

Heat 90 g/3 oz butter in a frying-pan with the oil. Dust the steaks with the flour and fry briefly on both sides. Remove and reserve the meat. Add the onion and garlic to the pan with the wine, stock, bayleaf, basil and half the parsley and season with salt. Simmer for 15 minutes. Return the meat to the pan and simmer for a further 30 minutes.

Serve with the mushrooms, sautéed in the remaining butter and parsley.

OSSOBUCO

Serves 6

100 g/3$^{1/2}$ oz butter
6 pieces ossobuco (veal knuckle)
2 tbsp flour
1 onion, peeled and finely chopped
3 garlic cloves, finely chopped
peel of 1 lemon, finely chopped
100 ml/3$^{1/2}$ fl oz white wine

Top: Entrecote Chasseur
Bottom: Hake and Cockles

3 tomatoes, skinned, seeded and chopped
250 ml/9 fl oz chicken stock
1 tbsp chopped sage
salt

Heat the butter in a flameproof casserole. Dust the meat with flour and brown all over. Add the onion, garlic and lemon peel and cook until lightly coloured. Add the wine and simmer to reduce. Stir in the tomatoes, stock, chopped sage and season with salt, cover and cook slowly for about 1¼ hours. Add more stock occasionally, if necessary.

Serve with white rice.

VEAL MARENGO

Serves 5

550 g/1¼ lb stewing veal, diced
salt
pepper
60 ml/2 fl oz oil
1 onion, peeled and finely sliced
4 garlic cloves, finely chopped
250 g/9 oz ripe tomatoes, skinned, seeded and chopped
8 tbsp red wine
100 ml/3½ fl oz chicken stock
1 tsp thyme
1 bayleaf
1 tbsp chopped parsley
100 g/7 oz button mushrooms
250 g/9 oz shallots, peeled

Season the meat with salt and pepper and brown in hot oil in a flameproof casserole. Add the sliced onion and garlic and cook for a few minutes, then add the tomatoes, wine and stock and cook for 10 minutes. Stir in the meat, chopped thyme, bayleaf and parsley, cover and cook for about 1 hour until the meat is tender. Meanwhile, sauté the mushrooms and shallots together in a frying-pan and add to the casserole when the meat is cooked. Serve very hot.

POACHED EGGS ON BRIOCHES

Serves 5

5 eggs
salt
8 tbsp wine vinegar
5 brioches
60 g/2 oz butter
100 g/3½ oz ham, diced
8 tbsp single cream
5 tsp mustard

Preheat the oven to 170° C/325° F, gas mark 3. Poach the eggs in boiling, salted water to which the vinegar has been added. Scoop out the crumb from the brioches, butter the insides and fill with the diced ham mixed with the cream. Place the poached eggs in the brioches and warm through for a few minutes in the oven. Remove and dot with a little mustard.

STEAK BOLOGNESE

Serves 5

5 rump steaks
salt
pepper
120 g/4 oz flour

2 eggs, beaten
60 g/2 oz fresh breadcrumbs
oil for frying
5 slices ham
5 slices Emmenthal cheese
100 ml/3½ fl oz fresh tomato sauce

Preheat the oven to 220° C/425° F, gas mark 7. Season and flour the steaks, coat with beaten egg and breadcrumbs and fry in hot oil. Cover each steak with a slice of ham and a slice of cheese, folded in two. Pour over the tomato sauce and heat through in the oven for 15 minutes.

**Top: Poached Eggs on Brioches
Bottom: Steak Bolognese**

Below: Cold Fillet Steak in Aspic
Opposite: Milanese Veal Chops

HAM WITH PINEAPPLE

Serves 6

1 x 1.5 kg/3¼ lb whole cooked ham
7 cloves
200 g/7 oz brown sugar
250 ml/9 fl oz grapefruit juice
3 slices pineapple
6 canned morello cherries, halved

Preheat the oven to 180° C/350° F, gas mark 4. Using a sharp knife, cut 7 small flaps in the ham, put a clove into each and rub the sugar all over. Place in a baking tin, pour over the grapefruit juice and roast in the oven for about 40 minutes. Remove and garnish with the pineapple slices and halved cherries. Return to the oven for 5 minutes. Serve with white rice or creamed potatoes.

MILANESE VEAL CHOPS

Serves 6

100 g/3¹/₂ oz grated Parmesan cheese
60 g/2 oz breadcrumbs
6 veal chops
120 g/4 oz flour
1 egg, beaten
oil for frying
150 g/5 oz macaroni
200 ml/7 fl oz fresh tomato sauce
200 ml/7 fl oz pint chicken stock
90 ml/3 fl oz Madeira
100 g/3¹/₂ oz button mushrooms, sliced
90 g/3 oz ham, finely chopped
100 g/3¹/₂ oz Serrano ham or coppa, finely
chopped

Mix half the cheese with the breadcrumbs.
Dust the chops in flour, coat with beaten
egg, then the breadcrumb mixture and fry
gently in hot oil for about 30 minutes,
turning once. Cook the macaroni in
boiling, salted water and drain. Place the
tomato sauce, stock, Madeira, mushrooms
and both hams in a casserole, cover and
cook for 10 minutes. Stir in the cooked
macaroni, heat through then remove from
the heat and add the remaining cheese.

Serve the macaroni and sauce in a deep
serving dish with the chops arranged on
top.

COLD FILLET STEAK IN ASPIC

Serves 8

1.5 kg/3¹/₄ lb beef fillet (in one piece)
salt
75 g/2¹/₂ oz lard
150 ml/5 fl oz Madeira
500 ml/10 fl oz aspic
1 small can foie gras
2 truffles, finely chopped
2 hard-boiled eggs, shelled and halved

Preheat the oven to 190° C/375° F, gas
mark 5. Tie the beef with string and rub
all over with salt. Heat the lard in a
roasting tin and lightly brown the beef all
over. Pour over the Madeira and roast in
the oven for 40 minutes, then remove
from the oven and allow to cool,
occasionally bathing in half-set aspic.

Make a paste with the foie-gras and
truffles. Brush several small moulds with
the liquid aspic, add the foie-gras paste and
fill with the remaining aspic, then leave to
set. Slice the cold fillet, sprinkle with diced
aspic and garnish with the foie-gras and
hard-boiled eggs. To turn out the foie-gras
from the moulds, stand in hot water for a
few minutes.

PARTY HORS D'OEUVRES

TOMATO MOUSSE

Serves 5

2 onions, peeled and finely chopped
1 tbsp oil
30 g/1 oz butter
700 g/1¹/₂ lb tomatoes, skinned, seeded and chopped
4 eggs, separated
1 tbsp flour
salt
pepper
2 tbsp dry sherry
4 gelatine leaves, soaked

Sauté the chopped onions in the oil and butter until soft, add the tomatoes and cook for 5 minutes. Liquidize in a blender then pour into a small mixing bowl. Add the egg yolks and the flour and cook over a pan of simmering water until thickened. Season with salt and pepper, and add the sherry and dissolved gelatine. Allow to cool, then beat the egg whites until stiff and fold in. Turn into a ring mould and refrigerate.

Invert the mousse on to a serving dish, fill with salad and garnish with stuffed hard-boiled eggs and asparagus, if desired.

LOBSTER SOUFFLE

Serves 6

1 x 500 g/1 lb 2 oz cooked lobster
90 g/3 oz butter
60 g/2 oz flour
500 ml/18 fl oz hot milk
salt & pepper
4 eggs, separated
2 truffles, finely chopped
60 g/2 oz Cheddar cheese, grated
250 g/9 oz cooked king prawns in shells

Carefully remove all the flesh from the lobster, including the claw meat.

Preheat the oven to 180° C/350° F, gas mark 4. Make a Béchamel sauce; melt 60 g/2 oz butter, add the flour and cook until lightly coloured, then pour on the hot milk. Season with salt and pepper and simmer for 5 minutes. Add the lobster pieces, the four egg yolks and the chopped truffles, stirring thoroughly. Beat the egg whites until stiff then fold into the mixture. Grease a soufflé dish with the remaining butter and pour in the mixture, sprinkle with the grated cheese, and cook in the oven for about 30 minutes.

Serve immediately, garnished with the prawns, peeled or unpeeled.

VICHYSOISSE

Serves 6

3 large leeks, chopped
1 medium onion, peeled and chopped
60 g/2 oz butter
300 g/10 oz potatoes, peeled and sliced
1 litre/1³/₄ pints chicken stock
250 ml/9 fl oz single cream
salt
pepper
1 spring onion, green part only, chopped

Sauté the leeks and onion for a few minutes in the butter, without browning. Add the potatoes and stock, cover and simmer for about 20 minutes, until the potatoes are cooked. Liquidize in a blender or food processor and refrigerate. Just before serving, stir in the cream, season with salt and pepper and garnish with the chopped spring onion.

POTATO GRATIN

Serves 6

1.5 kg/3¹/₄ lb potatoes, peeled and thickly sliced
salt & pepper
500 ml/18 fl oz milk
4 eggs, beaten
200 g/7 oz Emmenthal cheese, grated
1 tbsp finely chopped parsley
60 g/2 oz butter, diced

Place the sliced potatoes in a saucepan of cold, salted water. Bring to the boil, lower the heat and cook slowly for a few minutes, so that they are still slightly underdone. Drain thoroughly and arrange in an ovenproof dish.

Preheat the oven to 170° C/325° F, gas mark 3. Boil the milk and allow to cool slightly. Season the beaten eggs and add to the milk with half the grated cheese, some pepper and the parsley. Cover the potatoes with this mixture and dot with butter then sprinkle over the remaining cheese. Cook in the oven for 30 minutes. Brown under the grill just before serving.

EGGS A LA CREME

Serve 6

75 g/2¹/₂ oz butter
2 tbsp flour
500 ml/18 fl oz milk
60 ml/2 fl oz dry sherry
1 small can truffles, finely sliced, liquid reserved
250 g/9 oz button mushrooms, diced
100 g/3¹/₂ oz ham, diced
4 eggs, separated
salt
6 eggs

Make a thin Béchamel sauce; melt the butter, stir in the flour then add the hot milk. Bring to the boil, add the sherry, the reserved truffle liquid, diced mushrooms and ham, finely sliced truffles and simmer for 10 minutes.

Preheat the oven to 220° C/425° F, gas mark 7. Remove the sauce from the heat and stir in the egg yolks. Season with salt, beat the egg whites until stiff and fold in. Meanwhile, poach the 6 eggs. Arrange them in an ovenproof dish and pour over the sauce. Brown in the oven for a few minutes and serve immediately.

Top: Vichyssoise
Bottom: Eggs á la Creme

CHEESE PATTY WITH TOMATO SAUCE

Serves 6

100 g/3¹/² oz butter
150 g/5 oz flour
750 ml/1¹/⁴ pints hot milk
100 g/3¹/² oz Gruyère cheese, diced
100 g/3¹/² oz grated Parmesan cheese
3 eggs, separated
salt & pepper
breadcrumbs
250 ml/9 fl oz fresh tomato sauce

Make a thick Béchamel sauce; melt the butter, stir in the flour then add the hot milk and simmer for 10 minutes. Add the cheeses away from the heat, then add the egg yolks. Beat the egg whites until stiff and fold in. Season with salt and pepper.

Preheat the oven to 180° C/350° F, gas mark 4. Butter an ovenproof dish, sprinkle with breadcrumbs then pour in the mixture. Bake in the oven for 30 minutes. Serve hot with tomato sauce and fried bread, if desired.

CREAM OF PRAWN SOUP

Serves 6

500 g/l lb 2 oz cooked prawns
2 tbsp oil
1 garlic clove, finely chopped
1 leek, finely chopped
1 carrot, peeled and finely chopped
1 small onion, peeled and finely chopped
60 ml/2 fl oz brandy
3 tbsp flour
100 ml/3¹/² fl oz white wine
3 tbsp fresh tomato sauce
100 g/3¹/² oz butter
1 egg yolk
salt & pepper

Peel the prawns, mash the shells in a mortar with a little hot water and strain the juice. Reserve. Heat the oil in a saucepan and soften the garlic, leek, carrot and onion. Pour in the brandy, warm gently over a low heat, ignite and shake the pan until the flames die down. Stir in the flour and cook for a few minutes then pour in the wine, tomato sauce and 1.5 litres/2¹/² pints boiling water. Add the prawns, strained prawn juice and half the butter and simmer for 5 minutes. Just before serving, combine some of the hot liquid from the pan with the egg yolk and stir back into the pan with the remaining butter, to thicken the soup. Season with salt and pepper and serve immediately.

CREAM OF MARROW SOUP

Serves 6

1 kg/2¹/⁴ lb marrow, peeled and chopped
2 litres/3¹/² pints chicken stock
30 g/1 oz butter
salt & pepper

Place the chopped marrow in a saucepan with the stock. Bring to the boil, cover and simmer until the marrow has almost disintegrated. Remove from the heat and add the butter. Liquidize in a blender or food processor, season with salt and pepper and serve hot.

TRUFFLE TART

Serves 6

For the pastry:
60 g/2 oz butter
120 g/4 oz flour
3 tbsp water
pinch salt

For the filling:
30 g/1 oz butter
45 g/1¹/² oz flour
500 ml/18 fl oz hot milk
3 hard-boiled eggs, shelled and chopped
200 g/7 oz button mushrooms, sliced and cooked
2 large truffles, finely sliced
salt & pepper
7 canned artichokes, chopped

To make the pastry, rub the butter into the flour until it resembles fine crumbs. Make a well in the centre, add the water and salt then work together and knead gently into a smooth ball of dough. Leave to stand for 30 minutes. Meanwhile, preheat the oven to 180° C/350° F, gas mark 4. Roll out the dough and use to line a flan tin. Prick the base all over and bake in the oven for 20 minutes until golden.

For the filling, make a Béchamel sauce; melt the butter, stir in the flour then add the hot milk and simmer for 10 minutes. Stir in half the chopped eggs, half the mushrooms and one truffle, reserving the rest as a garnish. Season and pour the filling into the pastry case then return to the oven for 15 minutes. Remove and garnish with the artichokes and remaining chopped eggs, mushrooms and truffle. Serve very hot.

CHICKEN CONSOMME

Serves 6

500 g/1 lb 2 oz beef, diced
60 g/2 oz minced beef
1 calf's foot or 2 pig's trotters, cut in pieces
1 large onion, peeled and coarsely chopped
1 large carrot, peeled and coarsely chopped
2 tomatoes, skinned, seeded and chopped
1 celery stalk
1 tbsp chopped parsley
salt
1 chicken quarter

This consommé is a clear, refined stock, more concentrated than a basic stock.

Place all the ingredients except the chicken into a large saucepan of cold water and season with salt. Bring to the boil and cook gently, uncovered, for 2 hours, skimming off the froth. Allow to cool, add the chicken quarter and cook for a further hour. Allow to cool.

To clarify the consommé: when cold, add 2 egg whites to the consommé. Stirring continuously, bring to the boil then immediately add a few spoonsful of cold water. Boil again for a few minutes. Strain through muslin dampened with cold water. Add a glass of dry sherry (about 60 ml/2 fl oz).

Royals: this is the name given to the various small savoury custards traditionally served with a consommé. Preheat the oven to 180° C/350° F, gas mark 4. Beat together 2 eggs and a yolk as if for an omelette. Add 8 tablespoons of boiling stock. Strain into individual buttered moulds. Cook in the oven in a bain-marie for about 20 minutes. When cold, cut into pieces and serve.

Top: Chicken Consommé
Bottom: Basque Txangurro (recipe on page 59)

MAIN COURSES FOR PARTIES

YORK HAM IN PORT

Serves 4

4 x 120 g/4 oz slices York ham
salt
pepper
1 tbsp cornflour
45 g/1½ oz butter
120 ml/4 fl oz port
8 tbsp orange juice

Season the ham with salt and pepper and coat lightly with the cornflour. Place in a flameproof dish. Melt the butter and add the port and orange juice. Pour over the ham and cook very gently for 10 minutes, until the sauce thickens. Serve with creamed or new potatoes.

**Top: York Ham in Port
Bottom: Poached Eggs with Chicken Liver Pâté**

POACHED EGGS WITH CHICKEN LIVER PATE

Serves 8

8 eggs
pinch salt
1 tsp vinegar
8 slices bread
100 g/3½ oz chicken liver pâté
pinch nutmeg
250 g/9 oz cooked spinach
60 g/2 fl oz fresh tomato sauce, heated

Poach the eggs in boiling water, with salt and vinegar added. Toast the bread and mix the pâté and nutmeg into the spinach. Spread the mixture on the toast, making a hollow in the centre of each. Place a poached egg in each hollow and pour over the hot tomato sauce.

SAVOURY MUSHROOM CUSTARDS

Serves 6

6 eggs
250 ml/9 fl oz milk
100 g/3½ oz ham, chopped
salt
pepper
500g/1 lb 2 oz button mushrooms
90 g/3 oz butter
250 ml/9 fl oz Béchamel sauce
6 slices fried bread

Garnish:
120 g/4 oz whole button mushrooms sautéed in butter

Preheat the oven to 180° C/350° F, gas mark 4. Beat the eggs and mix with the milk and chopped ham. Season with salt and pepper. Use 30 g/1 oz of the butter to grease 6 individual moulds, pour in the mixture and cook in the oven in a bain-marie for 20 minutes until the custard sets.

Chop half the mushrooms and slice the rest then sauté in the remaining butter. Add the chopped mushrooms to the Béchamel sauce. Arrange the fried bread on a dish, place a custard on each and pour on the sauce. Put piles of fried, sliced mushrooms between them and garnish with the whole button mushrooms.

CHICKEN WITH APPLES, PRUNES AND PINE NUTS

Serves 4

1 x 1.5 kg/3¼ lb chicken
salt & pepper
60 g/2 oz lard or butter
1 kg/2¼ lb apples, peeled and sliced
100 ml/3½ fl oz brandy
60 g/2 oz currants
100 g/3½ oz pine nuts

Preheat the oven to 200° C/400° F, gas mark 6. Season the chicken with salt and pepper and coat with the lard or butter. Place the sliced apples in the base of an ovenproof dish, put the chicken on top and pour over the brandy. Roast in the oven for about 1 hour until cooked and golden. Ten minutes before the end of cooking time add the currants and pine nuts. Serve straight from the dish.

TOURNEDOS HENRY IV

Serves 8

8 beef fillet tournedos
salt & pepper
120 g/4 oz flour
8 slices bread, fried

For the Béarnaise sauce:
4 tbsp wine vinegar
1 tbsp chopped tarragon
1 tbsp chopped chervil
1 tbsp finely chopped onion
3 egg yolks
100 g/3½ oz clarified butter

Season the tournedos with salt and pepper, dust with flour and fry over a high heat in very little oil. Put each steak on a piece of fried bread and serve in a pool of Béarnaise sauce.

For the Béarnaise sauce, place the vinegar in a saucepan with the chopped tarragon, chervil and onion. Simmer to reduce the liquid to 1 tablespoon. Add to the egg yolks in a bowl over a pan of simmering water and stir until thickened. Remove from the heat and stir in the clarified butter.

BASQUE TXANGURRO

Serves 6

2 cooked crabs
90 g/3 oz butter
1 onion, peeled and finely chopped
3 garlic cloves, finely chopped

100 ml/3½ fl oz brandy
250 ml/9 fl oz fresh tomato sauce
pinch cayenne
1 tsp mixed grain mustard
salt & pepper
8 tbsp double cream
2 tbsp fresh breadcrumbs
1 tbsp chopped parsley

Remove all the crab meat from the shells and reserve the shells. Preheat the oven to 220° C/425° F, gas mark 7. Melt 60 g/2 oz butter in a saucepan and gently fry the chopped onion and half the garlic. Add the crab meat, pour over the brandy and warm gently over a low heat. Ignite the brandy and shake the pan until the flames die down. Add the tomato sauce, cayenne to taste and mustard and season with salt and pepper. Simmer gently for about 5 minutes, stirring carefully.

Remove from the heat and add the cream. Pour the mixture into the cleaned crab shells, sprinkle with the breadcrumbs, chopped parsley and remaining garlic, dot with the remaining butter and brown in the oven for 5 minutes. Serve immediately.

Top: Chicken with Apples, Prunes and Pine Nuts
Bottom: Tournedos Henry IV

PARTY PUDDINGS

PINEAPPLE BAVAROIS

Serves 5

3 eggs
250 ml/9 fl oz milk
200 g/7 oz sugar
1 tbsp cornflour
1 gelatine leaf
4 canned pineapple rings, finely chopped
225 ml/8 fl oz double cream, whipped

Beat together the eggs, milk, sugar and cornflour. Cook gently until thickened then chill. Dissolve the gelatine in the reserved juice from the canned pineapple and stir in. Combine the cream and chopped pineapple, add to the mixture and pour into individual moulds. Chill until set. Turn out and serve with a raspberry coulis and garnish with whipped cream, pineapple and glacé cherries.

Above: Pineapple Bavarois
Opposite: Coffee Creme Caramel

PEARS WITH CREAM

Serves 6

6 dessert pears
500 g/1 lb 2 oz sugar
250 ml/9 fl oz white wine
pinch cinnamon

2 cloves
6 tbsp apricot jam
500 ml/18 fl oz double cream, whipped
60 g/2 oz flaked almonds

Peel the pears without removing the stalks.
Place in a flameproof casserole, cover with
water and add the sugar, wine, cinnamon
and cloves. Bring to the boil, cover and
cook for 20 minutes until tender. Leave to
cool in the cooking juices. Remove and
drain well. Coat the pears with the apricot
jam and place in individual sundae glasses
or arrange on a serving dish. Garnish with
the whipped cream and flaked almonds.

COFFEE CREME CARAMEL

Serves 6

200 g/7 oz sugar
5 eggs
500 ml/18 fl oz milk
4 tbsp strong black coffee
300 ml/10 fl oz double cream, whipped

To caramelize the moulds, dissolve 60 g/2
oz sugar in a little water. Simmer until a
golden syrup forms and use this to coat the
bases of 6 individual moulds. Preheat the
oven to 180° C/350° F, gas mark 4. Beat
together the eggs and the remaining sugar.
Boil the milk with the coffee, remove
from the heat and beat into the egg
mixture. Pour into the moulds and cook
in a bain-marie in the oven for 30 minutes
until set. Chill, turn out and decorate
with the whipped cream.

APPLE SOUFFLÉ
Serves 6

1 kg/2.2 lb apples
500 ml/18 fl oz milk
2 eggs, separated
6 tbsp sugar
2 tbsp cornflour
Liqueur: 1 small glass of Cointreau

Peel and core the apples and cut them into large slices. Put them in an ovenproof dish and sprinkle with 2 tablespoons of sugar and the Cointreau. Cook in a hot oven for 10 minutes. Remove from the oven and put to one side.

Heat the oven to 350° F/180° C, gas mark 4.

Put the milk and the rest of the sugar into a pan and bring to the boil. Remove from the heat and add the cornflour dissolved in the 2 egg yolks and 2 tablespoons of cold milk. Put the pan back on the heat and simmer for 10 minutes, stirring constantly. Remove from the heat. Beat the egg whites into stiff peaks and fold into the egg and milk mixture. Cover the apples with this mixture and cook in the oven for 35-40 minutes until golden. Serve warm.

APPLE TART

Serves 6

Pastry:
250 g/8 oz flour
60 g/2½ oz sugar
60 g/2½ oz butter
1 egg
3 tbsp milk

Crème patissière:
250 ml/9 fl oz milk
100 g/4 oz sugar
3 egg yolks
1tbsp cornflour
25 g/1 oz butter

1 apple, chopped finely

To make the pastry, place the flour on a pastry board and make a well in the centre. Add the other pastry ingredients and knead to form a dough. Leave to stand for a few minutes.

For the filling, bring the milk to the boil and combine all the other crème patissière ingredients in a separate pan. Add the boiling milk to the other ingredients a little at a time. Put this pan back on the heat and simmer until the mixture thickens, stirring constantly. Leave to cool slightly.

Set the oven to 400° F/200° C, gas mark 6.

Roll out the dough to form a circle and place this circle on a greased baking tray. Spread the cooled crème patissière on the pastry and sprinkle over the chopped apple and a tablespoon of sugar. A small glass of Kirsch can also be sprinkled over if desired. Cook in the oven for approximately 40 minutes until the pie is crisp and brown.

BANANAS WITH LIQUEUR AND CREAM

Serves 6

6 bananas, sliced lengthways
75 g/3 oz butter
150g/6 oz sugar
juice of 2 lemons
50g/2 oz currants
1 small glass rum
double or whipping cream

Melt the butter over a gentle heat; add the sugar, lemon juice, rum and currants and let the mixture boil for about 5 minutes. Add the bananas and let them simmer in the mixture for a little while.

Serve with the cream in a separate dish.

LEMON PIE

Serves 6

Pastry:
150g/6 oz flour
75g/3 oz butter
50g/2oz sugar
1 egg yolk
1 tbsp milk
pinch cinnamon
salt

Filling:
80g/3 oz cornflour
200g/8 oz sugar
500 ml/18 fl oz water
8 tbsp lemon juice
grated rind of 3 lemons
3 egg yolks
40g/1½ oz butter

Make the pastry by combining all the ingredients together and put into a circular cake tin. Prick the pastry and cover with aluminium foil. Cook in a moderately hot oven for about 20 minutes.

For the filling, mix the sugar with the cornflour, add the water and bring to the boil. Cook for a few minutes until the mixture thickens, then remove from the heat, add the lemon juice, lemon rind and the egg yolks, one by one, and beat the mixture well. Finally add the butter and continue beating until it is mixed thoroughly.

Remove the baked pastry from the cake tin and put the filling into the pastry case. Let the pie cool and decorate with cream or meringue.

PEACHES IN RED WINE
Serves 4

1 kg/2.2 lb peaches
75 g/3 oz sugar
500 ml/18 fl oz red wine
juice of 1 lemon
8 tbsp water
double or whipping cream
1 cinnamon stick

Put the wine, water, sugar, lemon juice and cinnamon stick in a pan, add the peaches (peeled or unpeeled) and simmer for approximately 20 minutes.

Serve at room temperature with the whipped cream in a separate dish.

LEMON MOUSSE

Serves 6

5 eggs, separated
150 g/6 oz sugar
double or whipping cream to decorate
juice of 3 lemons

Mix the egg yolks with the sugar and lemon juice. Put the mixture in a bain-marie and heat until it thickens. Remove from the heat. Beat the egg whites into stiff peaks and fold into the warm mixture.

Put into a serving dish and leave to cool. Then chill in the refrigerator. Decorate with the cream.

Top: Lemon Mousse
Bottom: Peaches in Red Wine

INDEX

Jack Johnson

SLEEP THROUGH THE STATIC

This book is printed on recycled paper. The CD *Sleep Through the Static* was recorded 100% on solar energy.

This book was approved by Jack Johnson

Photography by Thomas Campbell

Transcribed by Jeff Jacobson

Cherry Lane Music Company
Director of Publications/Project Editor: Mark Phillips
Manager of Publications: Gabrielle Fastman

ISBN: 978-1-60378-054-4

Visit our website at www.cherrylane.com

A LETTER FROM JACK:

To whom it may concern:

My friends and I have just finished recording a new album called Sleep Through the Static. *At this point in my life I weigh about 190 pounds and my ear hairs are getting longer. I also have a couple of kids. My wife popped them out, but I helped. Some of the songs on this album are about making babies. Some of the songs are about raising them. Some of the songs are about the world that these children will grow up in—a world of war and love, and hate, and time and space. Some of the songs are about saying goodbye to people I love and will miss.*

We recorded the songs onto analog tape machines powered by the sun in Hawaii and Los Angeles. One day, JP Plunier walked into the studio and told us, "It has been four to six feet and glassy for long enough," and so we gave him a variety of wind and rain as well as sun and so on. And Robert Carranza helped to put it all in the right places.

After inviting Zach Gill to join Adam Topol, Merlo Podlewski, and me on our last world tour, we decided to make him an official member of our gang. So our gang now has a piano player, which probably makes us much less intimidating, but Merlo, our bass player, is six-foot-three, so we are still confident.

All of these songs have been on my mind for a while and it is nice to share them. I am continually grateful to my wife, who is typing this letter as I dictate it to her.

I hope you enjoy this song book.

Mahalo for listening,

Jack Johnson

CONTENTS

ALL AT ONCE

Words and Music by
Jack Johnson

4

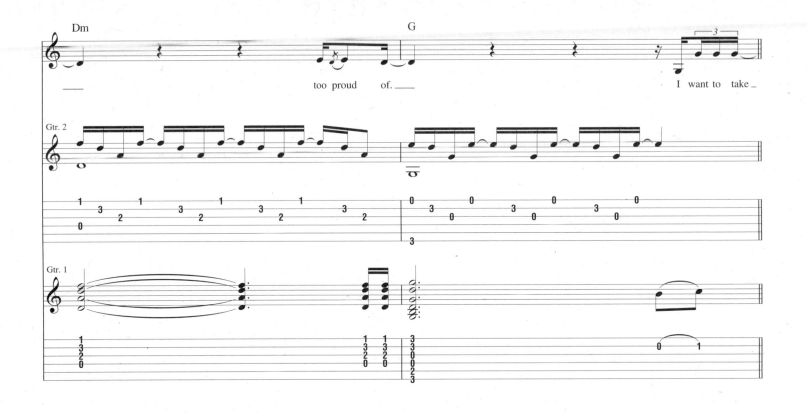

too proud of. ___   I want to take ___

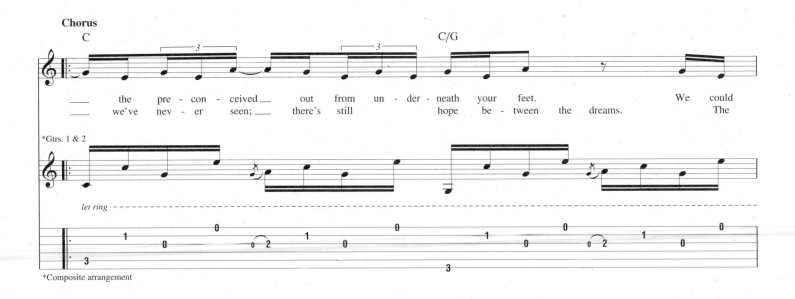

Chorus

___ the pre - con - ceived ___ out from un - der - neath your feet.   We could
___ we've nev - er seen; ___ there's still   hope be - tween the dreams.   The

*Gtrs. 1 & 2

let ring -

*Composite arrangement

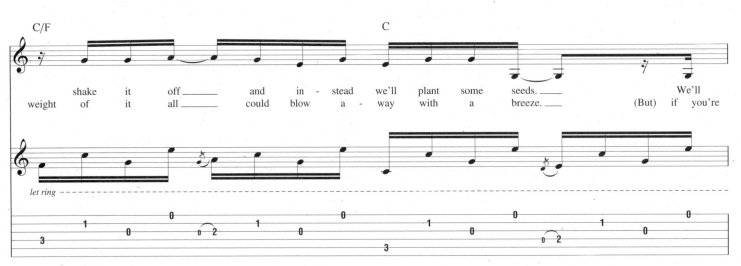

shake   it   off ___   and in - stead we'll plant some   seeds. ___   We'll
weight of it all ___   could blow a - way with a   breeze. ___   (But) if you're

let ring - - - - - - - - - - -

counts

What a - bout __ when it's gone?
What a - bout __ when it's gone?   Oh.   It real - ly won't be so   long. __   Some - times it

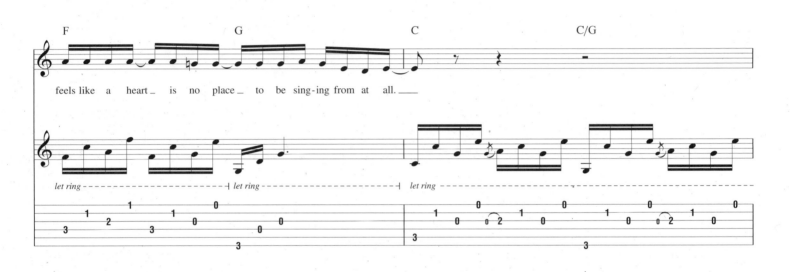

feels like a heart __ is no place __ to be sing-ing from at all. __

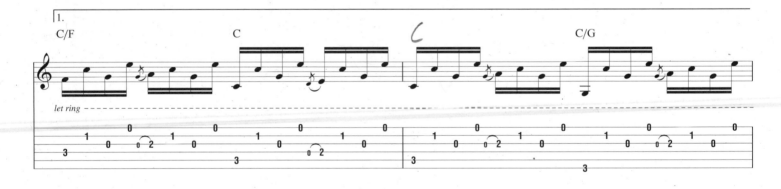

There's a   world __

8

SLEEP THROUGH THE STATIC

Words and Music by
Jack Johnson

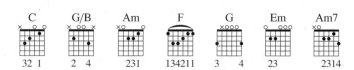

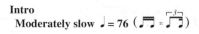

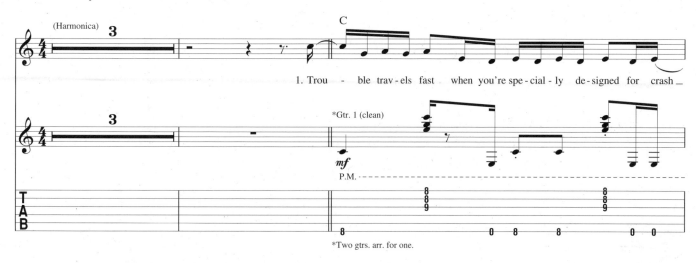

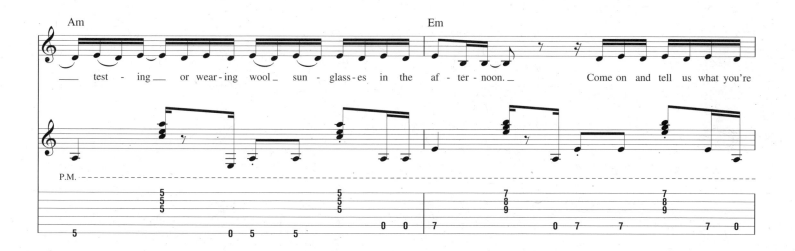

9

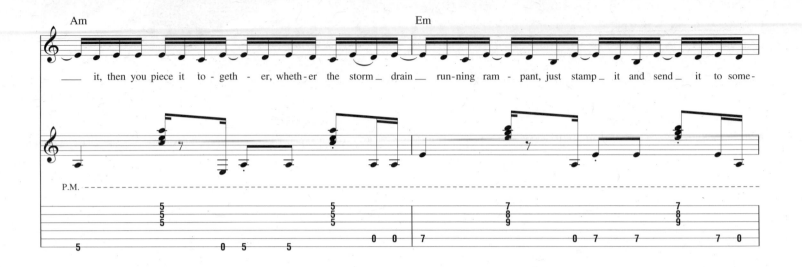

_ it, then you piece it to-geth-er, wheth-er the storm_ drain_ run-ning ram - pant, just stamp_ it and send_ it to some-

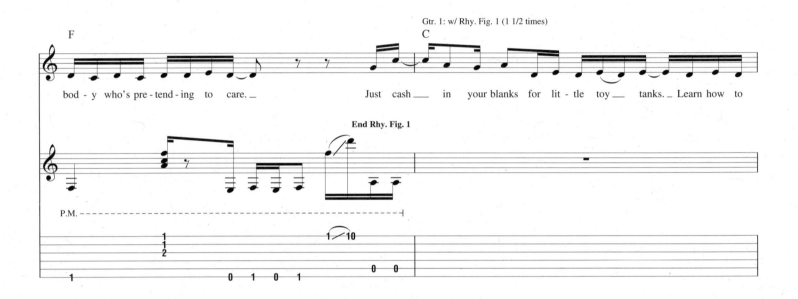

bod - y who's pre-tend-ing to care. _ Just cash_ in your blanks for lit - tle toy_ tanks. _ Learn how to

use them, then a - buse them and choose them o - ver con - ver - sa -

- tions. Re - la - tion - ships _ are o - ver - rat - ed. "I

hat - ed ev - 'ry - one," said the sun. And so I will

10

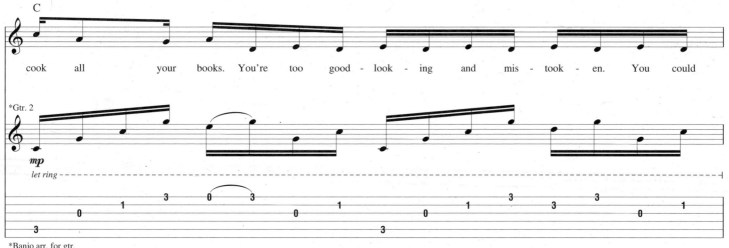

cook all your books. You're too good - look - ing and mis - took - en. You could

*Gtr. 2

mp

let ring

*Banjo arr. for gtr.

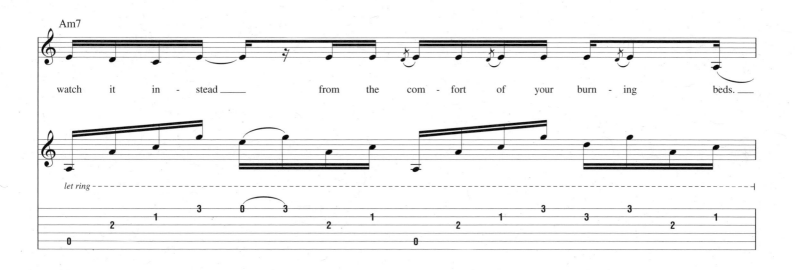

Am7

watch it in - stead ____ from the com - fort of your burn - ing beds. ____

let ring

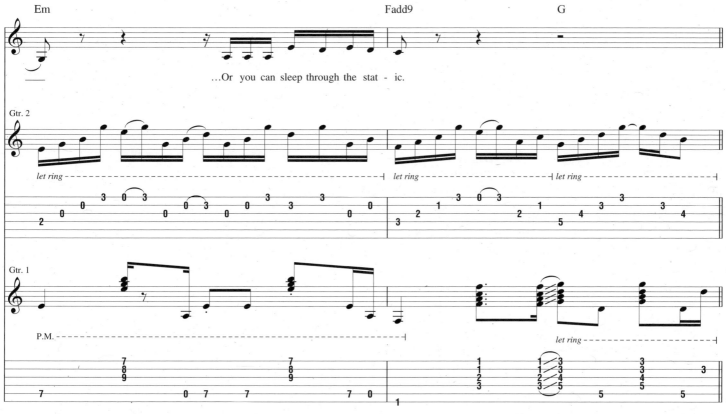

Em   Fadd9   G

...Or you can sleep through the stat - ic.

Gtr. 2

let ring ‑‑‑‑‑‑‑‑‑‑‑‑‑‑‑‑‑‑‑‑‑‑ let ring ‑‑‑‑‑‑‑‑‑‑‑‑‑‑‑‑ let ring ‑‑‑‑‑‑‑‑‑‑‑‑‑‑‑‑

Gtr. 1

P.M. ‑‑‑‑‑‑‑‑‑‑‑‑‑‑‑‑‑‑‑‑‑‑‑‑ let ring ‑‑‑‑‑‑‑‑‑‑‑‑‑‑‑‑‑‑

Chorus

Gtrs. 1 & 2 tacet

Who needs sleep when we've got love? Who needs keys when we've got clubs?

*Piano arr. for gtr.

Who needs please when we've got guns? Who needs peace when we've gone a-bove, but be-

yond where we should have gone? We went be-yond where we should have

Verse

Gtr. 1: w/ Rhy. Fig. 1 (3 1/2 times)
Gtr. 3 tacet

gone. 2. Stuck be-tween chan-nels, my thoughts all quit. I thought a-

bout them too much, al-lowed them to touch. The feel-ings that rained

Em ... F

_____ down on the plains _____ all dried and cracked wait-ing _____ for things that nev-er came. _____ Shock an

C ... Am

aw - ful thing to make some-bod - y think that they have to choose push-ing for peace, _ sup-port-ing the troops. And ei - ther you're weak _____

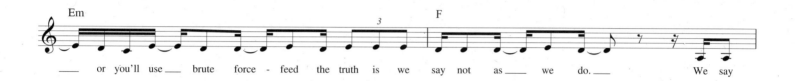

Em ... *3* ... F

_____ or you'll use _____ brute force - feed the truth is we say not as _____ we do. _____ We say

C

an - y - time, _____ an - y - where, just show your teeth and strike the fear of

*Gtr. 4

```
3                                                    5
```

*Horns arr. for gtr.

Am

God _____ wears _____ cam - ou - flage, _____ cries at night and drives a Dodge. _____

```
3                                                    5
```

Pick up the beat and stop hog-ging the feast. That's no way to treat an en-e-my.__ Well, might-y,

might-y ap-pe-tite, we just eat 'em up and keep on driv-ing. Free-dom can be freez-ing, take a pic-ture from the pret-ty side.

Mind your man-ners, wave your ban-ners. What a won-der-ful world__ that this an-gle can see.__

Gtr. 4

Gtr. 1

P.M. --

14

16

HOPE

Words and Music by
Jack Johnson and Zach Rogue

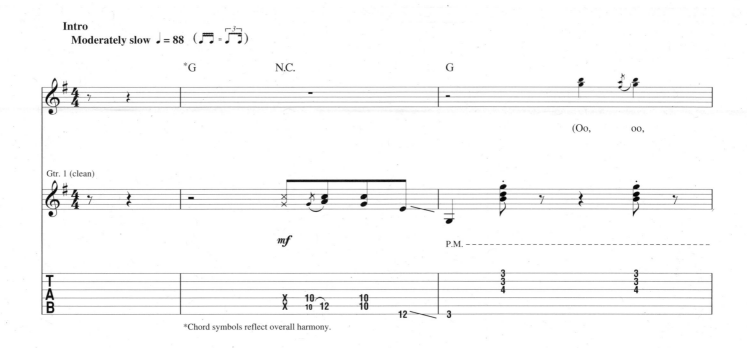

*Chord symbols reflect overall harmony.

(Oo,   oo,

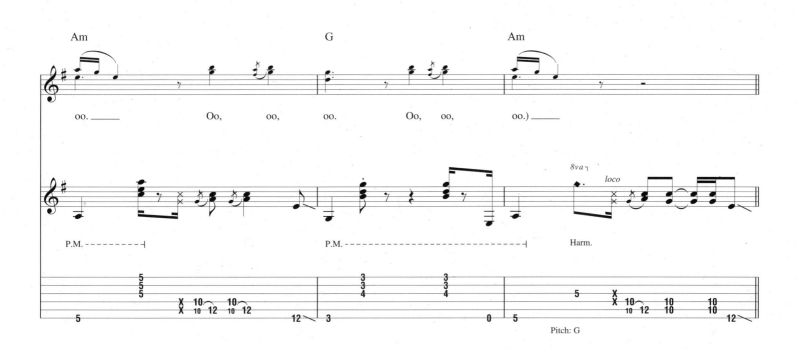

oo. _____ Oo,   oo,   oo.   Oo,   oo,   oo.) _____

Pitch: G

17

Verse

2nd time, Gtr. 2: w/ Riff A (4 times)

G ... Am

1. Your shad - ow walks fast - er than you. ___ You don't real - ly know what to
2. Your re - flec - tion is a blur, ___ out of fo - cus but in con -

Rhy. Fill 1 ... End Rhy. Fill 1

P.M. -

2nd time, Gtr. 1: w/ Rhy. Fill 1

G ... Am

do. Do you think that you're not a - lone? ___ You real - ly think that you're im -
fu - sion, the frames the sun did burn ___ at the end of a roll of de -

Rhy. Fill 2 ... End Rhy. Fill 2

P.M. -

G ... Am

mune to (it). It's gon - na get the best of you. ___ It's gon - na lift you up then
lu - sions, a ghost wait - ing its turn. ___ (And) now I can see right

P.M. -

Riff A

*Gtr. 2 (clean)

mf

w/ tremolo

*Kybd. arr. for gtr.

18

let you down. _____ Mm, mm, mm. _____ It will de -
through (it). It's a warn - ing that no - bod - y heard. _____ It will

Pre-Chorus

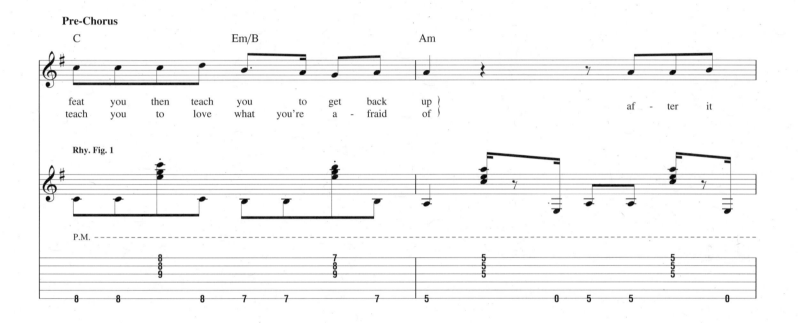

feat you then teach you to get back up
teach you to love what you're a - fraid of
af - ter it

Rhy. Fig. 1

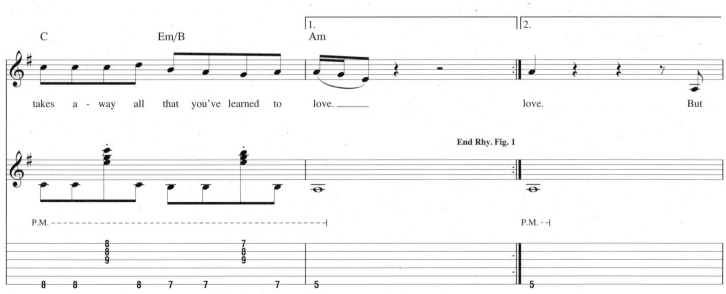

takes a - way all that you've learned to love. _____ love. But

End Rhy. Fig. 1

*Piano arr. for gtr.

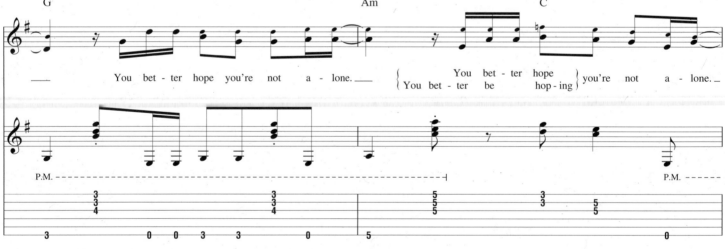

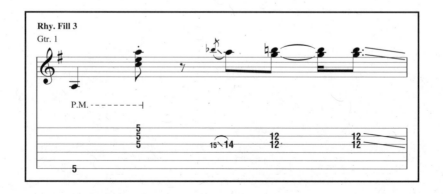

21

Verse

Gtr. 2: w/ Riff A (4 times)
Gtr. 4: w/ Riff B

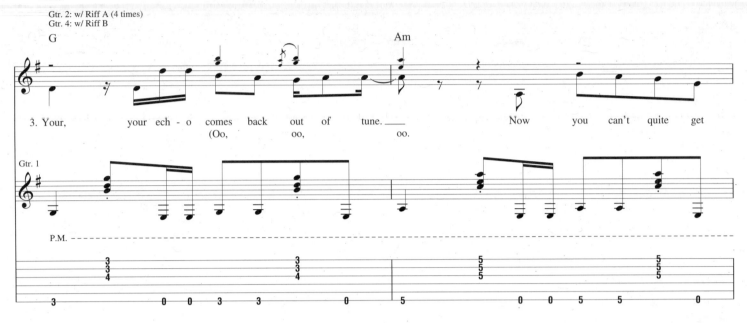

3. Your, your ech - o comes back out of tune. ___ Now you can't quite get
(Oo, oo, oo.

Gtr. 1

P.M. -

used to it. Re - verb is just the room. ___ The prob-lem is ___ that there's ___ no
Oo, oo, oo.

P.M. -

truth to (it). It's fad - ing a - way too soon. ___ Your shad - ow is on the move, ___
Oo, oo, oo.

P.M. -

Pre-Chorus

Gtr. 1: w/ Rhy. Fig. 1

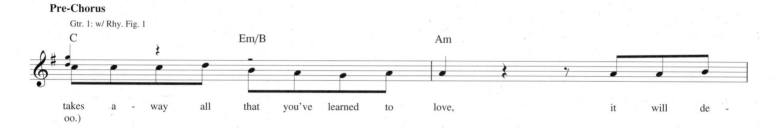

takes a - way all that you've learned to love, it will de -
oo.)

feat you then teach you to get back up. _____ 'Cause

Gtr. 3: w/ Rhy. Fig. 2

D.S. al Coda

you don't al - ways have to hold your head ___ high - er than your

Coda

Outro

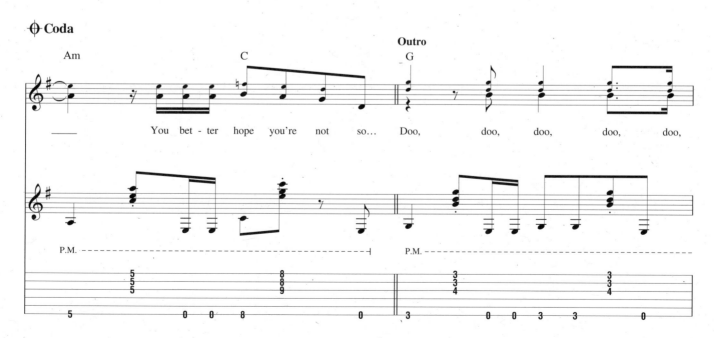

_____ You bet - ter hope you're not so... Doo, doo, doo, doo, doo,

ANGEL

Words and Music by
Jack Johnson

Capo III

Intro
Moderately slow ♩ = 92

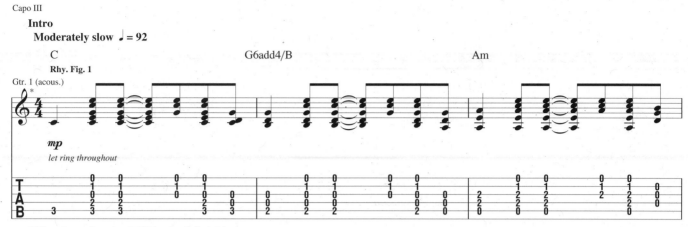

*All music sounds a minor 3rd higher than indicated due to capo.

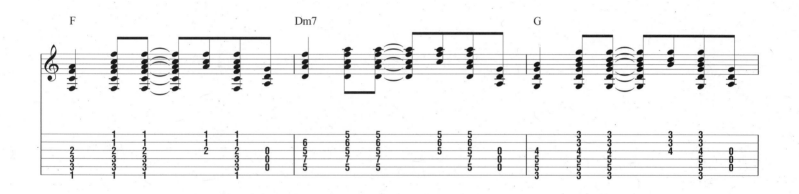

Verse
Gtr. 1: w/ Rhy. Fig. 1

- gel; she does - n't wear an - y wings. ___

She wears a heart ___

___ that could melt my own; ___ she wears a smile ___ that could make me want to sing. ___

___ 2. She gives me pres -

Verse
Gtr. 1: w/ Rhy. Fig. 1

- ents with her pres - ence a - lone. ___

She gives me ev - 'ry thing I could wish ___ for; she gives me kiss -

- es on the lips just for com - ing ___ home. 3. She can make

Verse
Gtr. 1: w/ Rhy. Fig. 1 (1st 7 meas.)

an - gels; (I've) seen it with my ___ own ___ eyes. ___

You've got to be care - ful when you've got good love, 'cause them an -

-gels will ____ just keep ____ on mul - ti - ply - ing.

Outro

But you're so bus - y chang - ing the world. ____

Gtr. 1

Just one smile ____ and you could change all of mine. ____

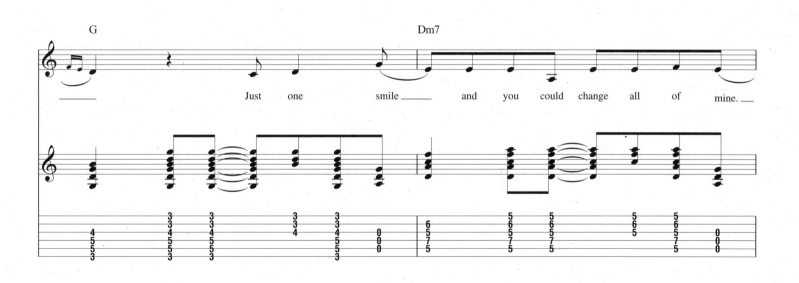

We share the same ____ soul. Oh, oh, oh, oh. ____

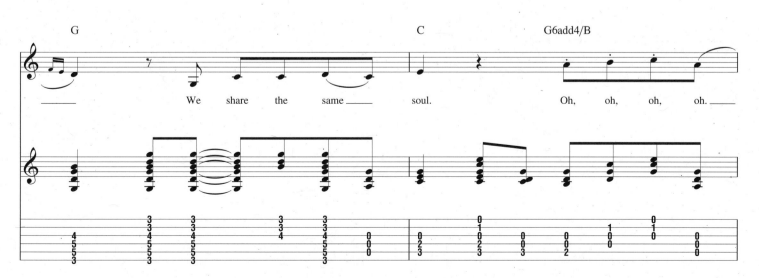

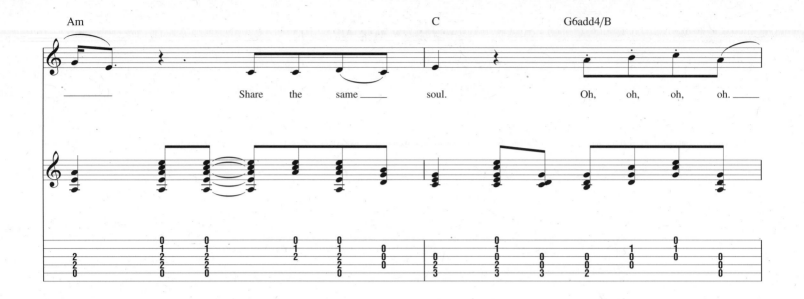

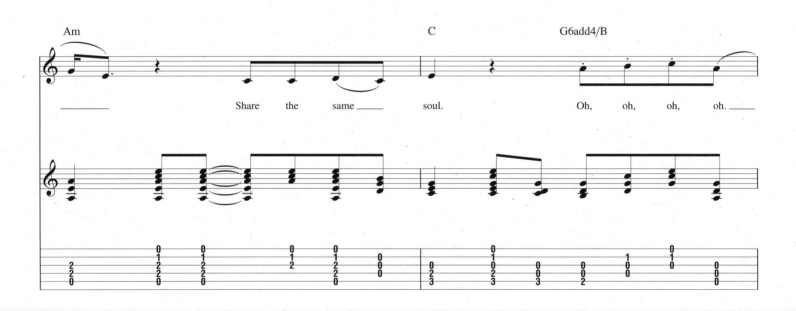

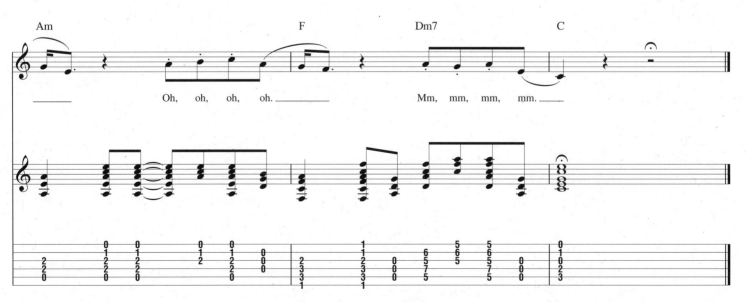

ENEMY

Words and Music by
Jack Johnson

Drop C tuning:
(low to high) C-A-D-G-B-E

Intro
Moderately ♩ = 120

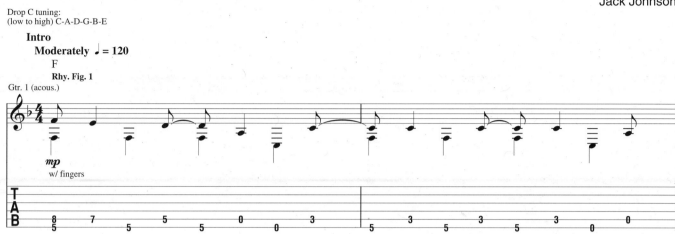

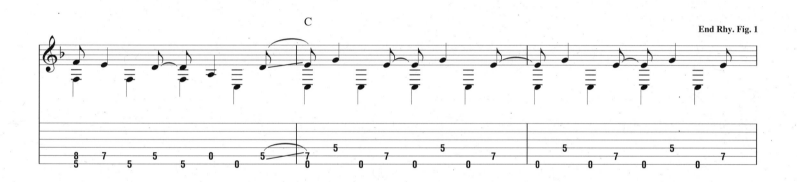

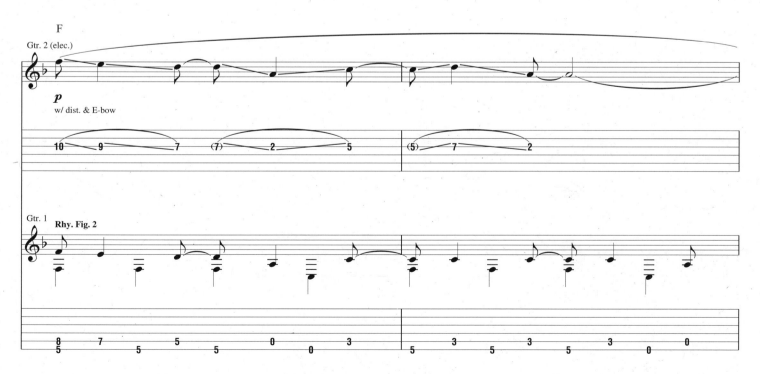

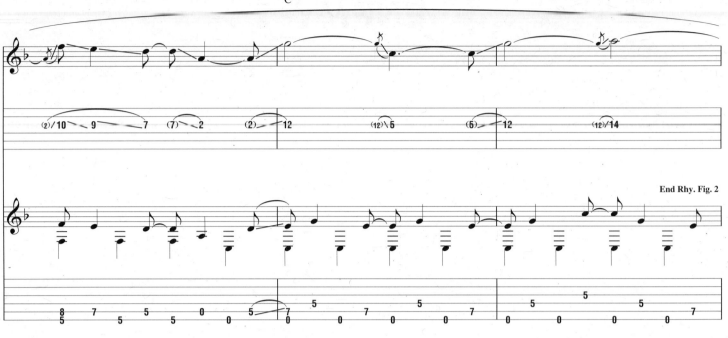

C

End Rhy. Fig. 2

Gtr. 1: w/ Rhy. Fig. 1

F

Gtr. 2

mp

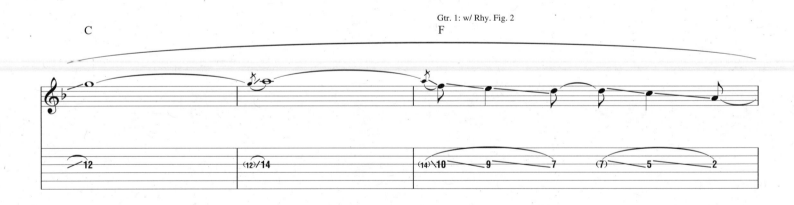

C

Gtr. 1: w/ Rhy. Fig. 2

F

C

fdbk.

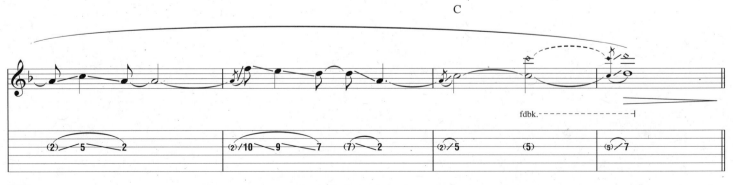

Verse

Gtr. 1: w/ Rhy. Fig. 2
Gtr. 2 tacet

F

1. Af - ter we spoke ____ I had a dream ____ that I broke ____ the
picked up the piec - es when ____ I woke ____ up. (I
blew on the sail, ____ watched it drift ____ out to sea. ____ The

C

teeth from a mouth ____ of a snake. ____ Then I choked ____ on the teeth; ____
put them in ____ a boat made of things ____ that I ____
fur - ther it drift - ed, the clos - er it came ____ to me; ____

Gtr. 1: w/ Rhy. Fig. 1
F

____ they were mine ____ all a - long. ____
____ don't want ____ to see. ____
____ I can't ex - plain. ____

| 1., 2. | 3. |

Verse

Gtr. 1: w/ Rhy. Fig. 2 (1st 4 meas.)

C   F

2. I
3. I

4. So I took it a - part, ____ built a bil -

C

- lion box - es, (but) there was on - ly one key. ____

𝄋 **Chorus**

B♭   C

You might think ____ I'm your ____ en - e - my, but

Gtr. 1

Rhy. Fill 1   **End Rhy. Fill 1**

31

IF I HAD EYES

Words and Music by
Jack Johnson

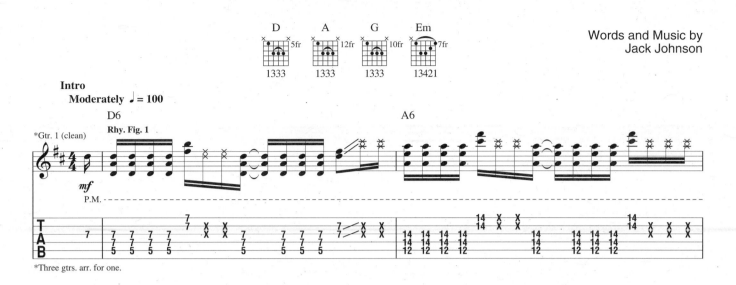

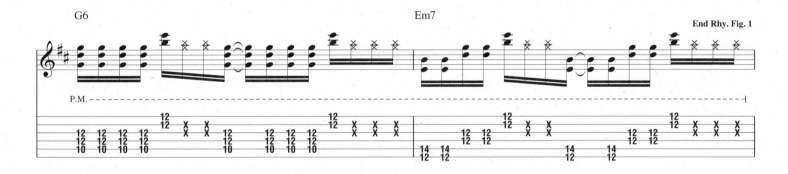

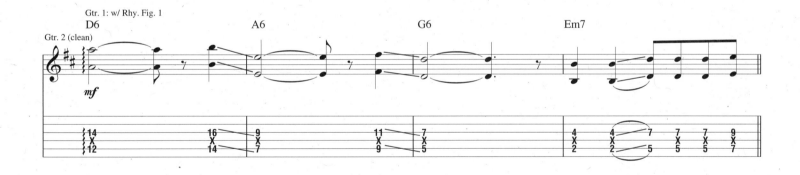

35

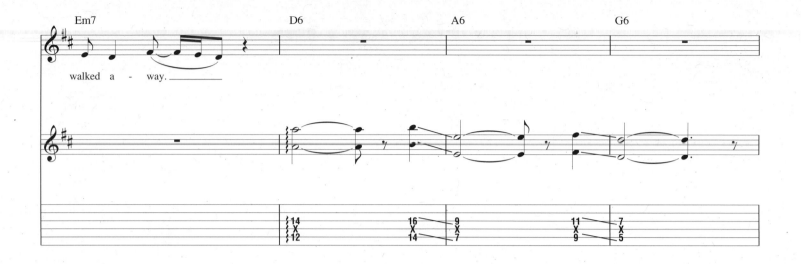

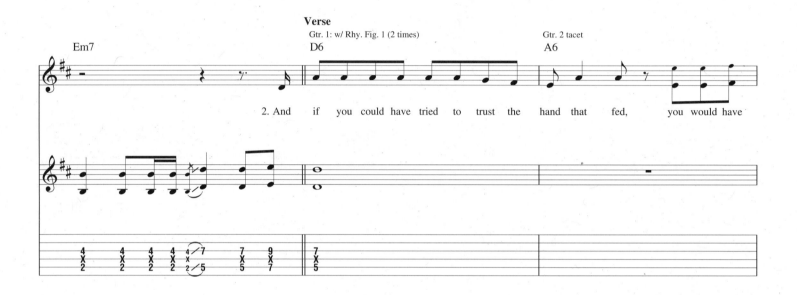

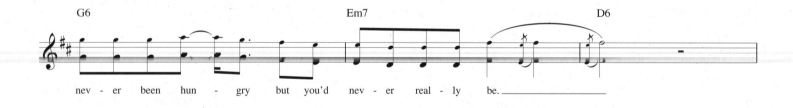

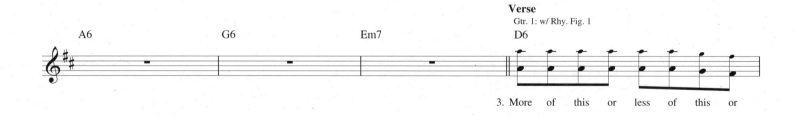

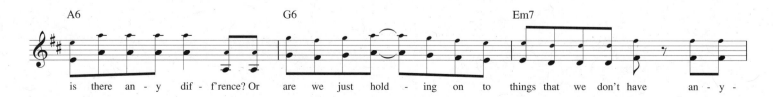

Interlude
Gtr. 1: w/ Rhy. Fig. 1 (2 times)

Al - ways _____ look - ing out. _____

(Oo, _____ oo, oo, oo, _____ oo. _____

Oo, _____ oo, _____ oo, oo, oo, _____ oo.)

4. A

Verse

lot of _____ peo - ple spend their time just _____ float - ing.

Rhy. Fig. 4

*Gtr. 3

*Piano arr. for gtr.

38

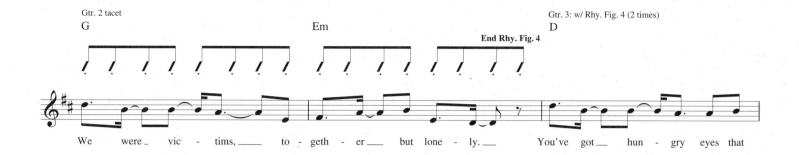

We were vic- tims, ___ to- geth- er __ but lone- ly. __ You've got __ hun- gry eyes that

just can't _ look for- ward. Can't give them _ e- nough but __ we just can't _ start o- ver.

Build- ing __ with bent nails, _ we're fall- ing __ but hold- ing. __ I don't _ want __ to take up

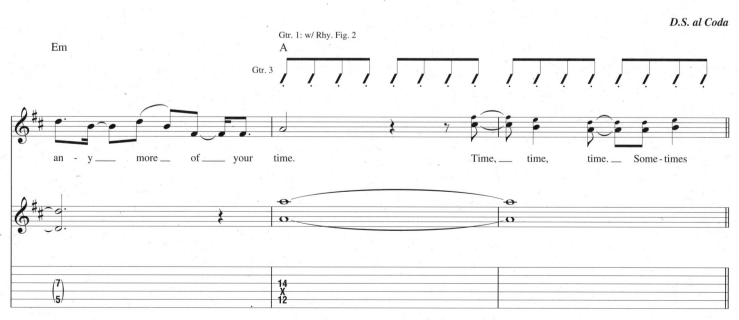

an - y __ more __ of __ your time. Time, __ time, time. __ Some- times

39

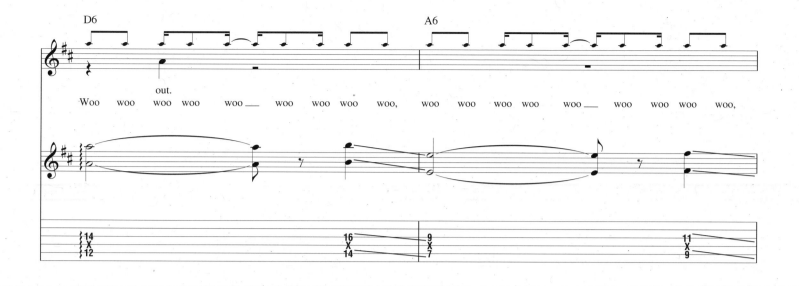

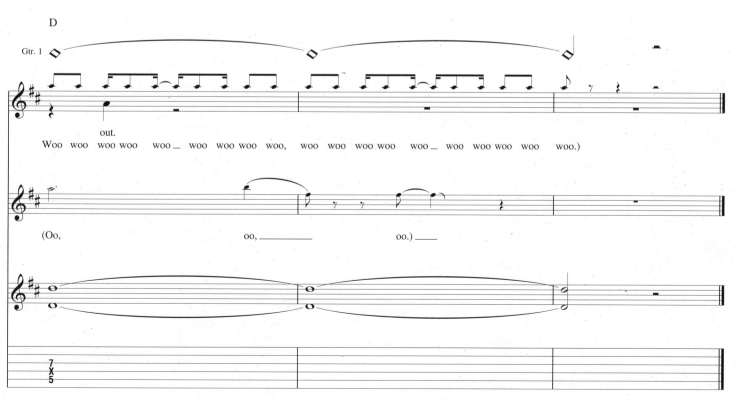

SAME GIRL

Words and Music by
Jack Johnson

Intro
Moderately ♩ = 120

Mm, _____ mm, mm, mm, _____ mm, mm, mm.

Verse
"Straight" feel

1. If you could read my ___ mind ___ you'd say, "Ba - by, you ___ were right ___

To Coda ⊕

Gtr. 1: w/*Rhy. Fig. 1

Mm, _____ mm, mm, mm, mm, mm, mm.

*w/ "straight" feel

Verse

Gtr. 1: w/ Rhy. Fig. 2 (3 times)

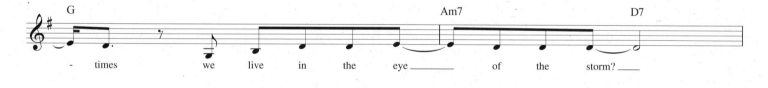

2. How can you be so _____ calm _____ when the truth _____ is that some -

- times we live in the eye _____ of the storm? _____

With ev - 'ry - thing _____ go - ing on a - round _____ us, I feel com - fort in the

sounds when you say it will be o - kay, like a

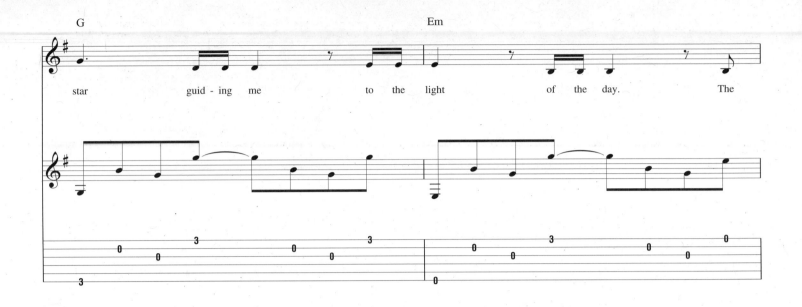

star   guid - ing me   to the light   of the day.   The

D.S. al Coda

dol - drums   could fol - low   me,_____   but not with my

⊕ **Coda**

Mm,_____   mm, mm, mm,_____   mm, mm, mm.

Gtr. 1

strum w/ thumb

WHAT YOU THOUGHT YOU NEED

Words and Music by
Jack Johnson

47

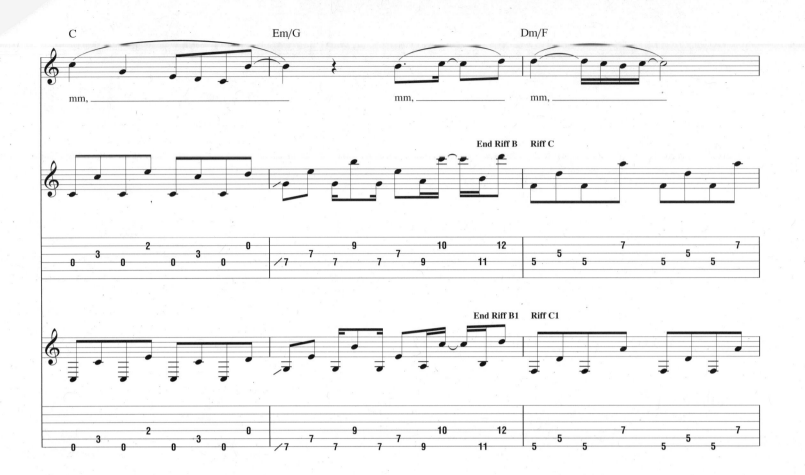

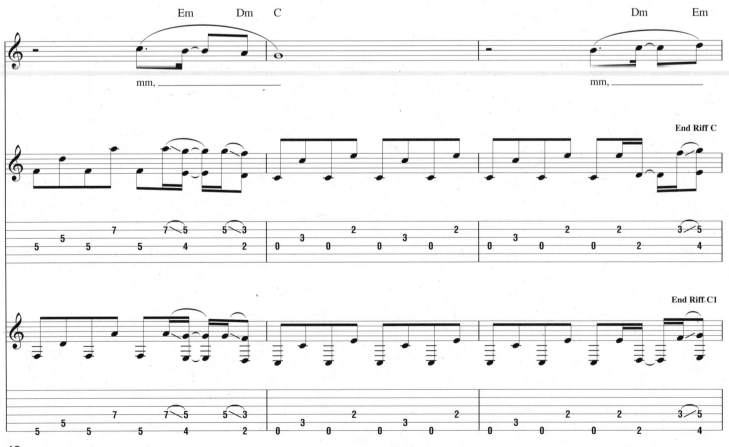

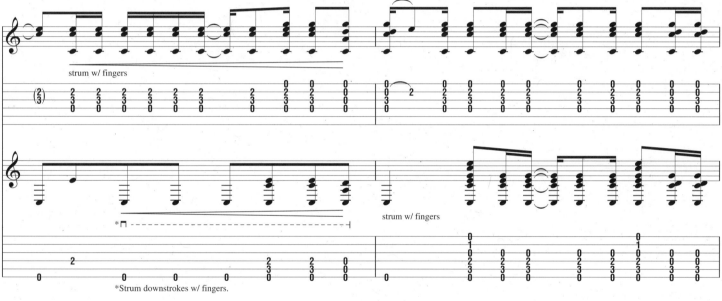

49

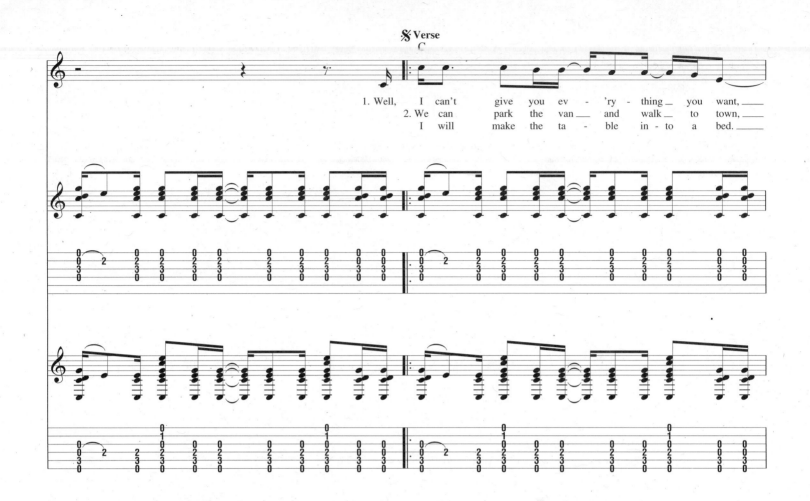

1. Well, I can't give you ev - 'ry - thing __ you want, __
2. We can park the van __ and walk __ to town, __
   I will make the ta - ble in - to a bed. __

__ but I could give __ you what you thought __ you need. __
find the cheap - est bot - tle of wine __ that we __ could find __
The can - dle is burn - ing down; __ it's time __ to rest. __

50

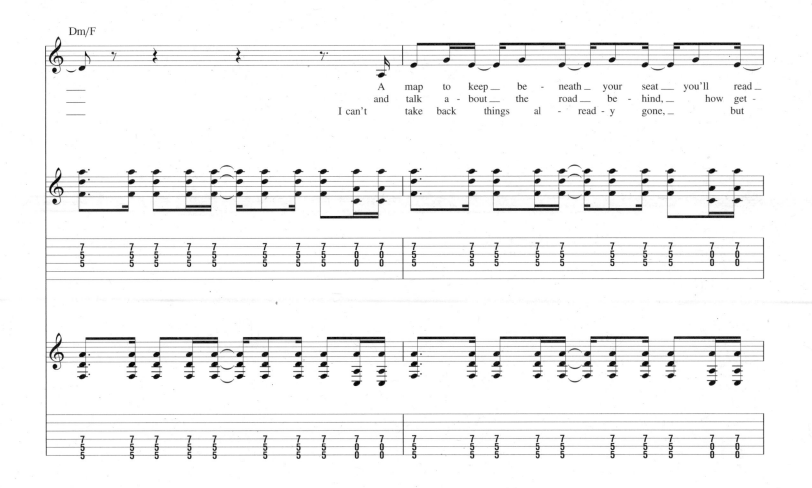

A   map   to   keep_   be - neath_   your   seat_   you'll   read_
and   talk   a - bout   the   road_   be - hind, _   how   get -
I   can't   take   back   things   al - read - y   gone, _   but

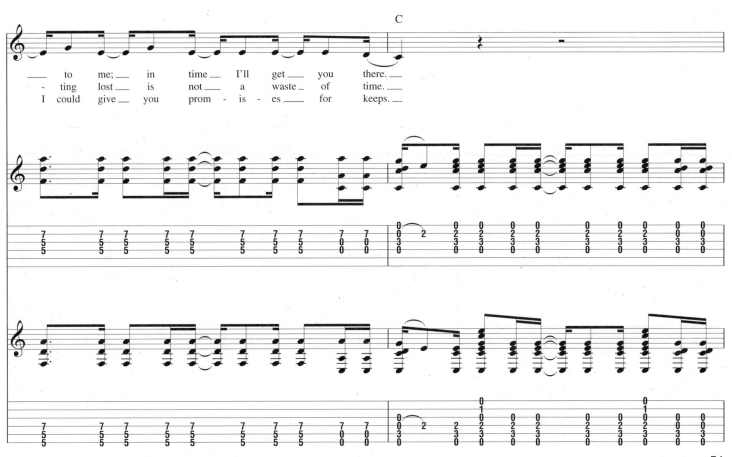

_   to   me; _   in   time_   I'll   get_   you   there. _
- ting   lost_   is   not_   a   waste_   of   time. _
I   could   give_   you   prom - is - es_   for   keeps. _

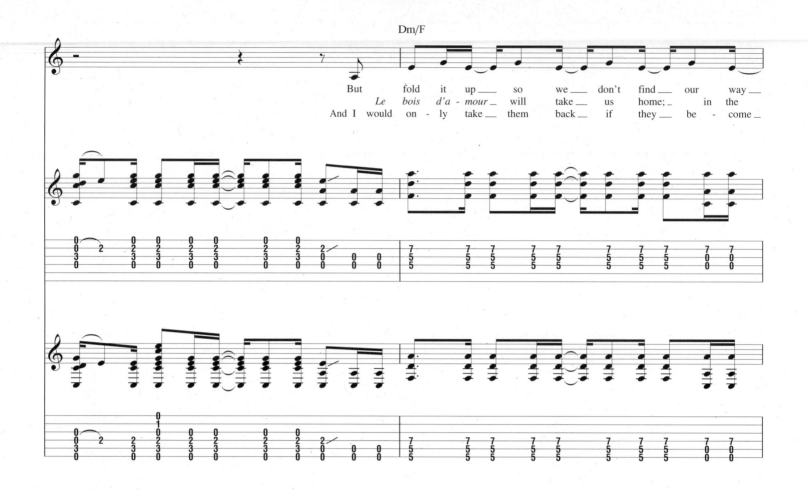

But   fold   it   up __ so   we   don't __ our   way __
Le   bois   d'a - mour __ will   take __ us   home;   in the
And   I   on - ly   take __ them   back   if   they __ be - come __

__ back   soon; __ no - bod - y   knows __ we're   here.
mo - ment   we __ will   sing __ as   the   for - est   sleeps. __
__ your   own __ and   you   give   them __ to   me.

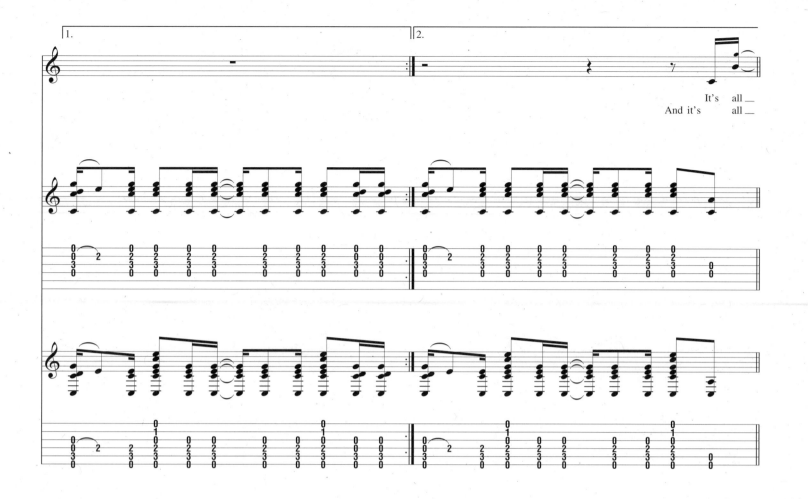

It's all ___
And it's all ___

Chorus

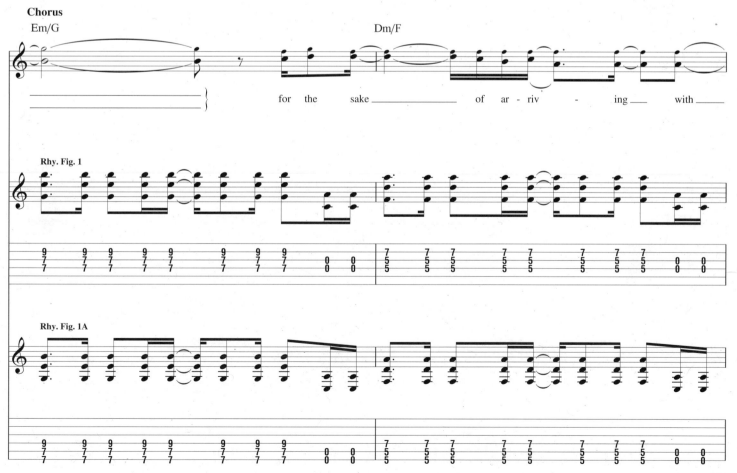

for the sake ___ of ar - riv - ing ___ with ___

Rhy. Fig. 1

Rhy. Fig. 1A

you.   Well, it's all

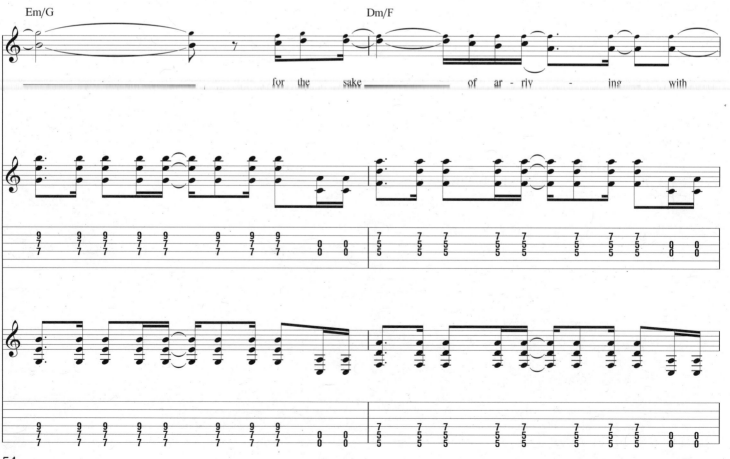

for the sake   of ar - riv   -   ing with

⊕ Coda

Gtrs. 1 & 2: w/ Rhy. Figs. 1 & 1A (2 1/2 times)

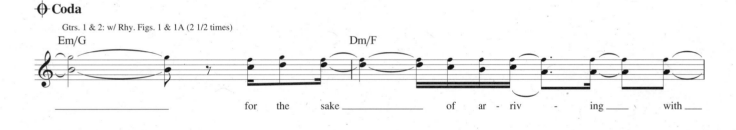

_____ for the sake _____ of ar - riv - ing ___ with ___

___ you.   We could make this in - to an - y - thing;   we could

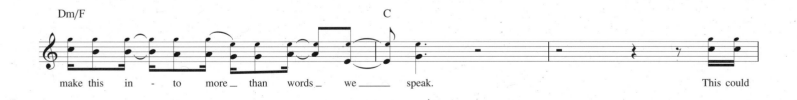

make this in - to more __ than words __ we _____ speak.   This could

make us in - to an - y - thing;   it could make us grow __ and be - come what __ we'll be. __

Outro
Gtr. 1: w/ Riff A
N.C.

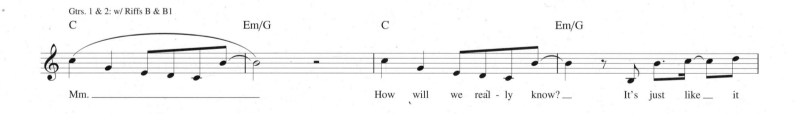

Gtrs. 1 & 2: w/ Riffs B & B1

C   Em/G   C   Em/G

Mm. _____   How will we real - ly know? __   It's just like __ it

Gtrs. 1 & 2: w/ Riffs C & C1 (1st 2 meas.)   Gtrs. 1 & 2: w/ Riffs A & A1

Dm/F   Em   Dm   N.C.

feels. _____   It's just like __ it feels.

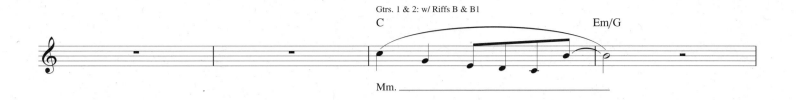

Mm. _____

How can we real-ly know? ___ It's just like ___ it feels. _____

It's just like ___ it feels. It's just like ___ it feels. _____

(Drums tacet)

How does ___ it feel? It's just like ___ it feels. _____

Begin fade

It's just like ___ it feels.

*Vocal and gtrs. only

How does ___ it feel? _____

It's just like ___ it feels. How does ___ it feel? _____

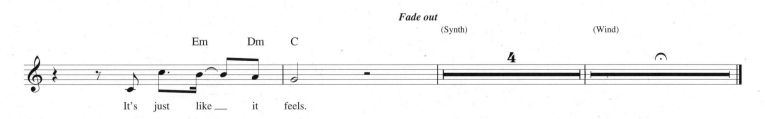

Fade out

(Synth)   (Wind)

It's just like ___ it feels.

ADRIFT

Words and Music by
Jack Johnson

Gtr. 2: Open F tuning:
(low to high) C-F-C-F-A-C

Intro
Moderately slow ♩ = 88

*Chord symbols reflect basic harmony.
**Downstemmed notes played w/ thumb; upstemmed notes strummed w/ fingers.

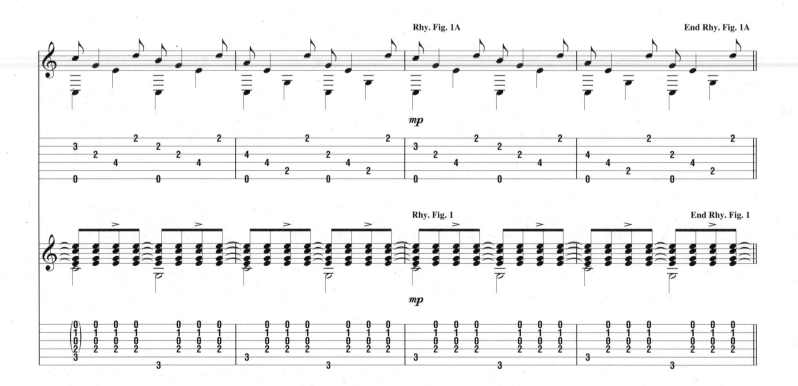

Verse

1. Your voice is a - drift; I____ can't ex - pect it to sing to me____ as

if I____ was the on - ly one.____ I'll fol - low__

you, _____ a leaf that's fol - low - ing the sun. _____

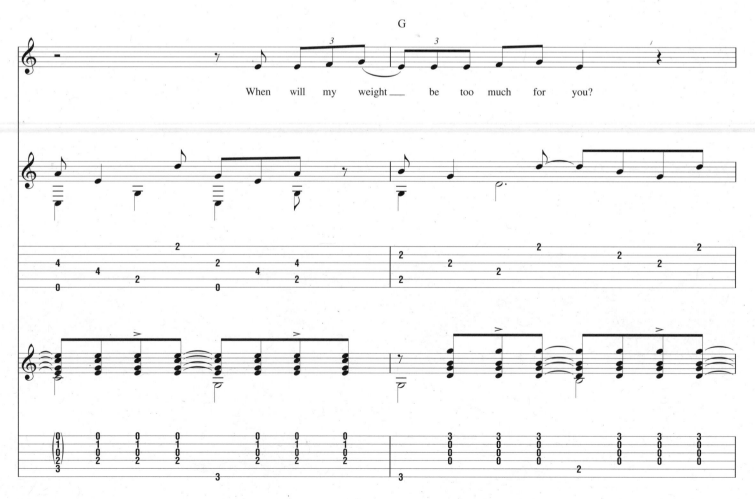

When will my weight _____ be too much for you?

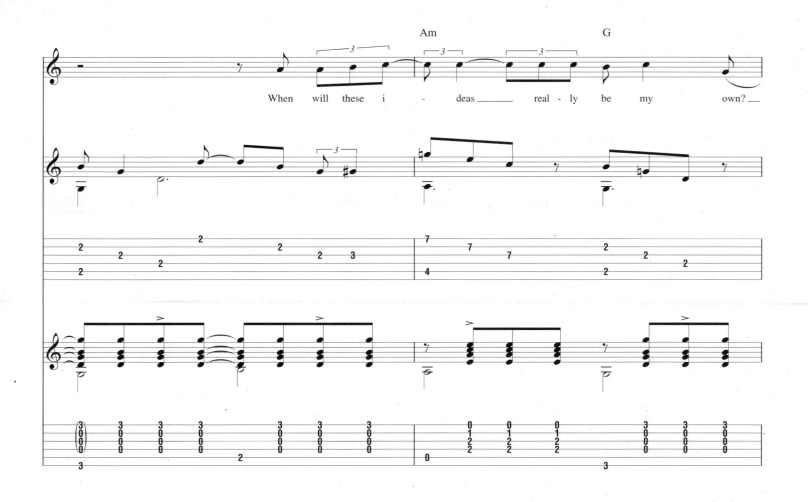

When will these i - deas really be my own?

'Cause this mo - ment keeps on mov - ing;

we were nev - er meant_ to hold on._

Verse

Gtrs. 1 & 2: w/ Rhy. Figs. 2 & 2A

2. (Well,) this was a scene worth_ wak - ing up for. When_ I _____ woke up, ____ you

*Gtr. 3

Riff A

*Mandolin arr. for gtr.

plant - ed me in my own pot. _____ (I) don't_ know_

why, _____ but some - how _____ it just feels so wrong. ____

When you set, _____ I will be lone - ly. But when you rise ___

__ a - gain, I'll have be - come __ the sun. ____ (And) I will shine down up - on you

as if you were ___ the on - ly one. ____

End Riff A

63

Verse

Gtrs. 1 & 2: w/ Rhy. Figs. 2 & 2A
Gtr. 3: w/ Riff A

C .... F

3. Your voice is your own; I ___ can't pro - tect it. You'll have to ___ sing ___ a

*Gtr. 4

*Mandolin arr. for gtr.

C

verse no one has ev - er known. ___ Don't be a -

F C

- fraid ___ 'cause no one ev - er sings a - lone. ___

G

Your weight will nev - er be too much for me. Your i - deas ___

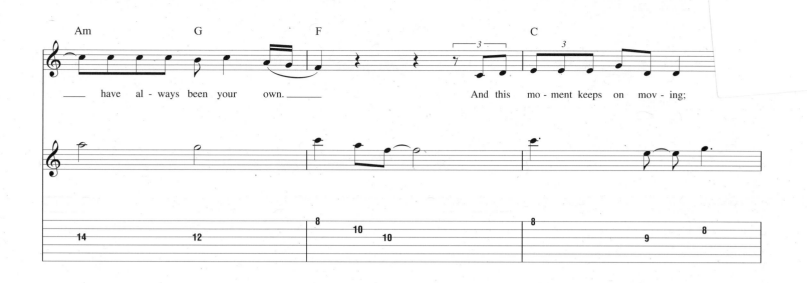

have al - ways been your own. And this mo - ment keeps on mov - ing;

we were nev - er meant to hold on.

Outro

Gtrs. 1 & 2: w/ Rhy. Figs. 1 & 1A

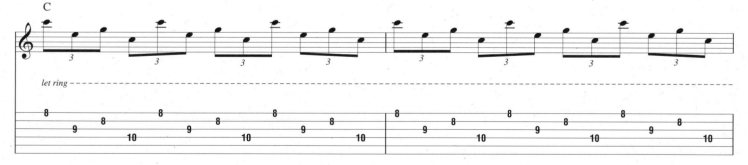

let ring -

Gtrs. 1 & 2: w/ Rhy. Figs. 2 & 2A (1st 15 meas.)

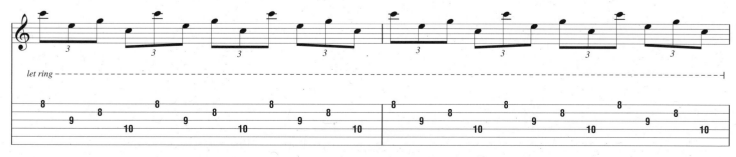

let ring -

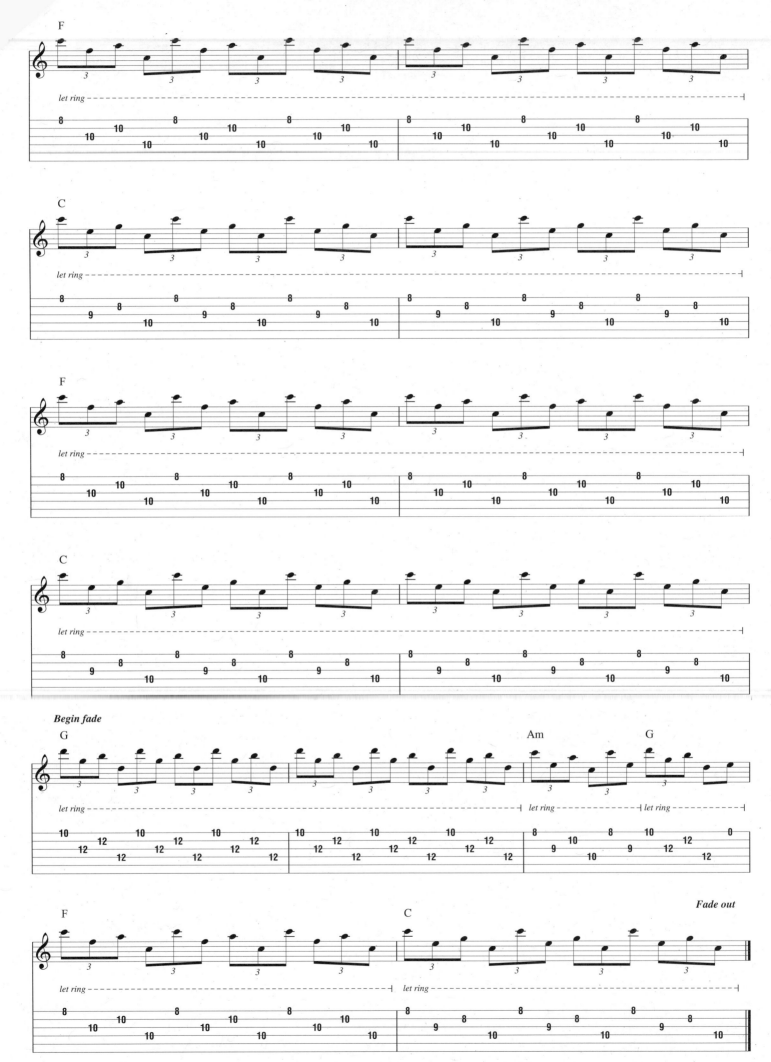

GO ON

Words and Music by
Jack Johnson

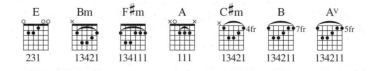

mo - ment that we start, _____   from the mo - ment that we start. _____

Interlude

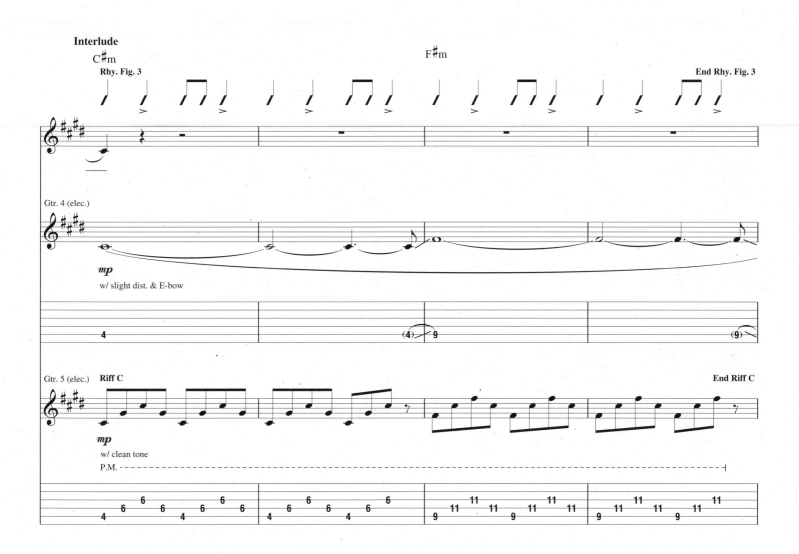

Gtr. 4 (elec.)

mp

w/ slight dist. & E-bow

Gtr. 5 (elec.) **Riff C**   **End Riff C**

mp

w/ clean tone

P.M. -|

Gtr. 1: w/ Rhy. Fig. 3
Gtr. 5: w/ Riff C

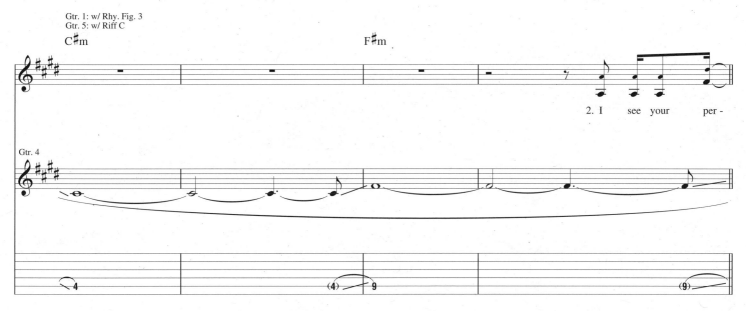

2. I   see   your   per -

Gtr. 4

Chorus

Gtr. 1: w/ Rhy. Fig. 2 (3 3/4 times)

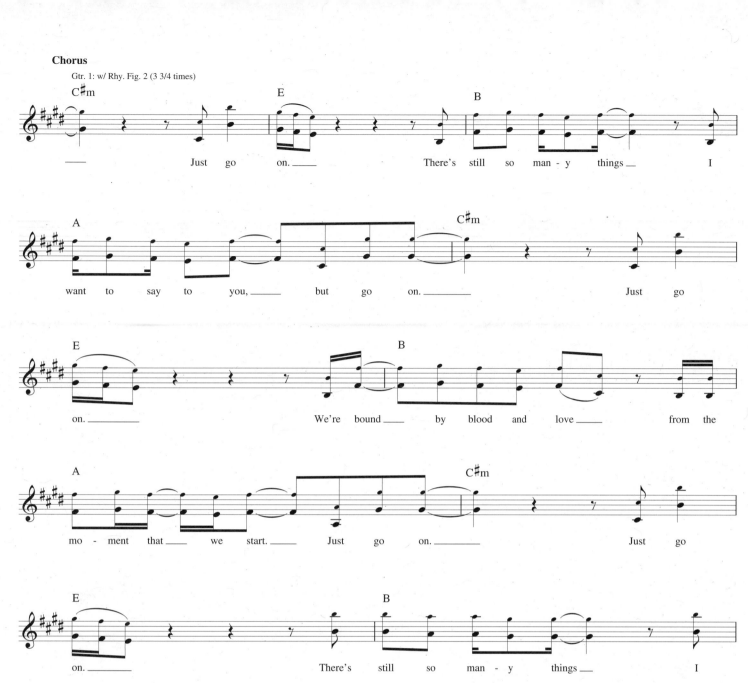

Just go on. ____ There's still so man-y things ___ I

want to say to you, ____ but go on. _____ Just go

on. _____ We're bound ___ by blood and love ___ from the

mo-ment that ___ we start. ___ Just go on. _____ Just go

on. _____ There's still so man-y things ___ I

want to say ___ to you. ___ Just go on. _____ Just go

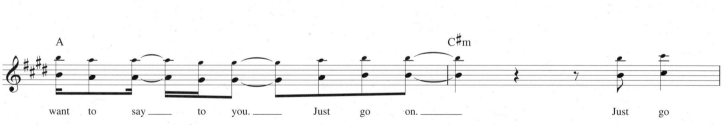

on. _____ We're bound ___ by blood that's mov-ing from the

Gtr. 1: w/ Rhy. Fill 1

mo-ment that we start, _____ from the mo-ment that we start. ____

Interlude

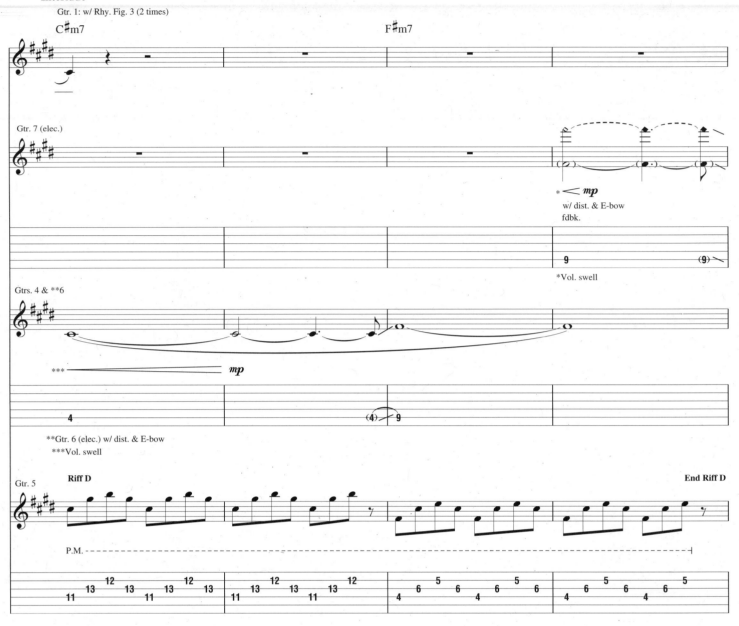

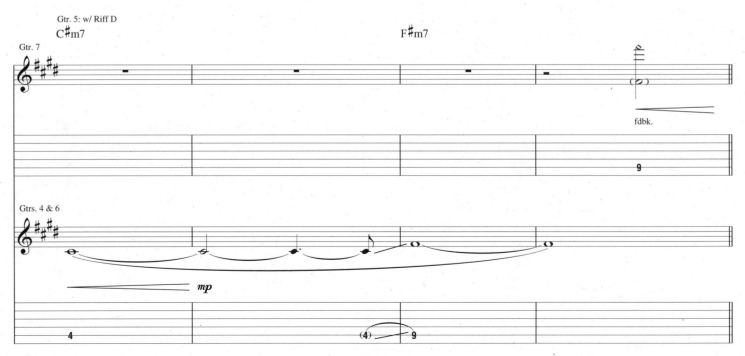

Outro

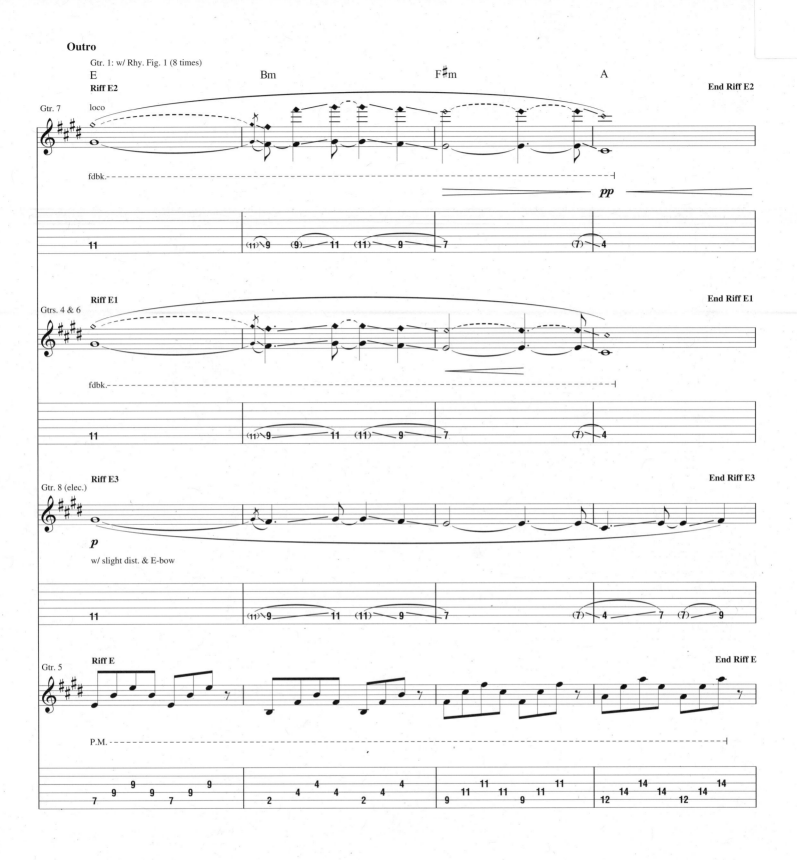

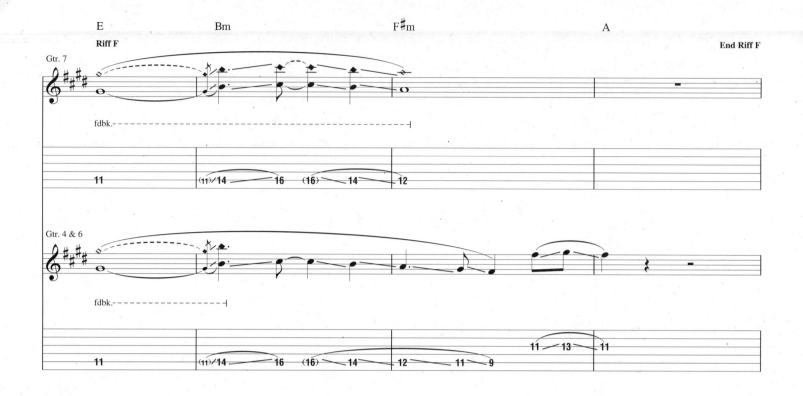

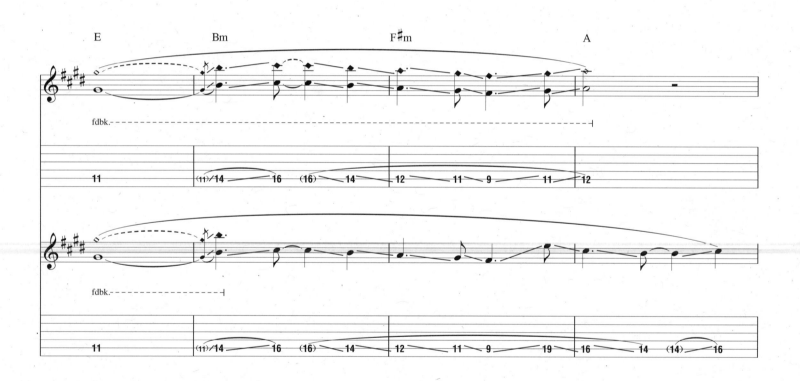

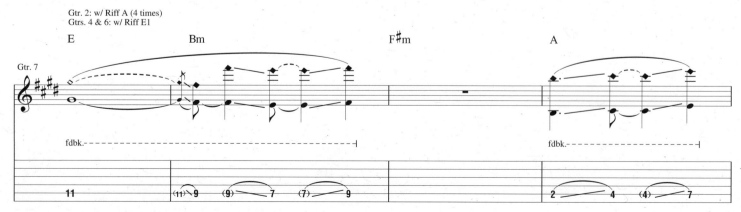

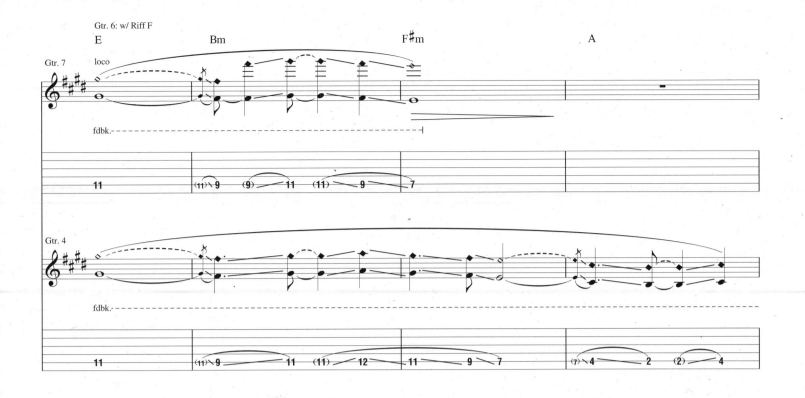

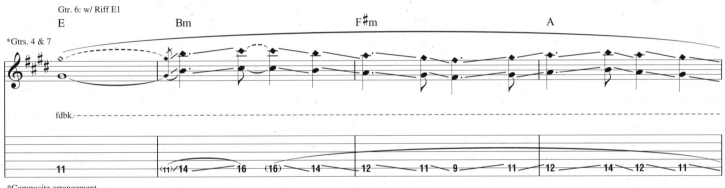

*Composite arrangement

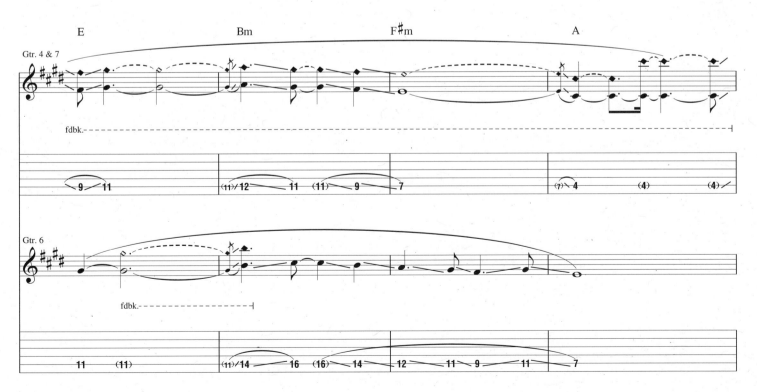

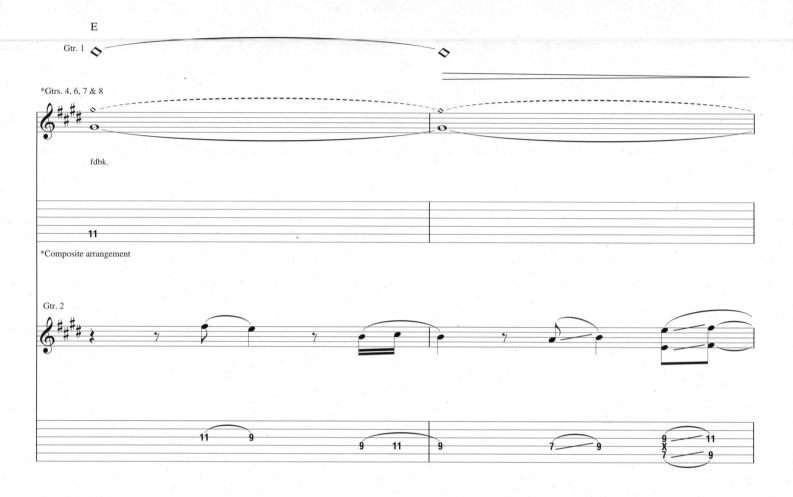

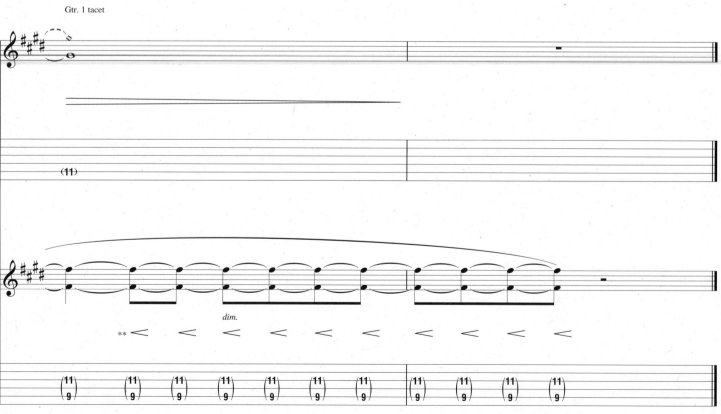

THEY DO, THEY DON'T

Words and Music by
Jack Johnson

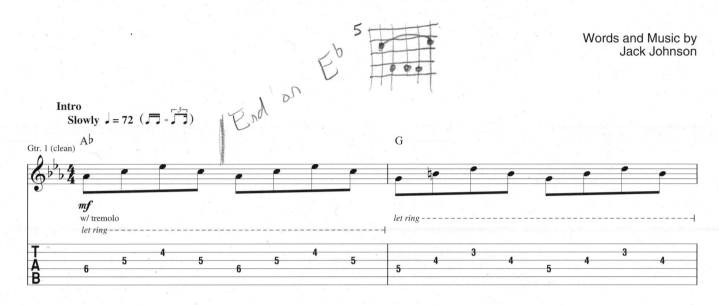

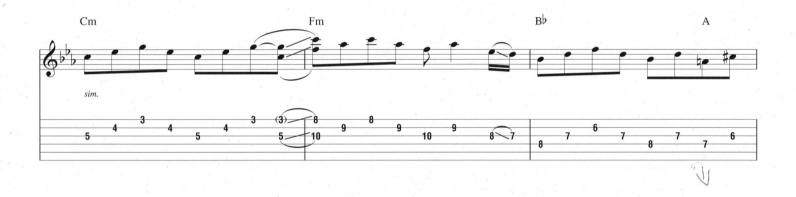

*Composite arrangement; Gtr. 2 (clean) w/ tremolo, played *mf*

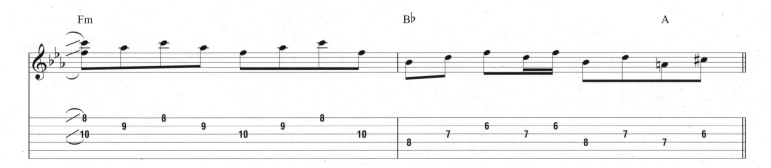

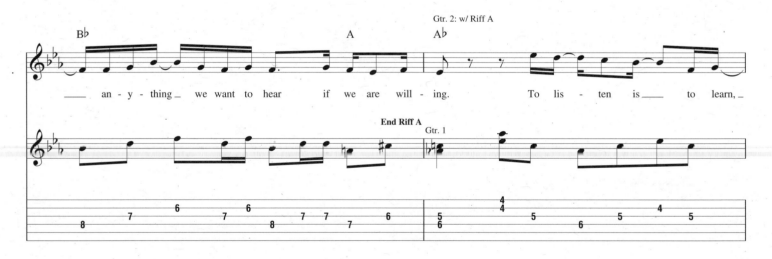

we don't? Pray to an - y - bod - y you want, ___ we won't. Oh, oh, oh, oh, oh, oh,

Chorus

oh.   But if we're the ones to blame, then the fruit ___ should - n't taste so good. We were u -

*Gtrs. 1 & 2

let ring

*Composite arrangement

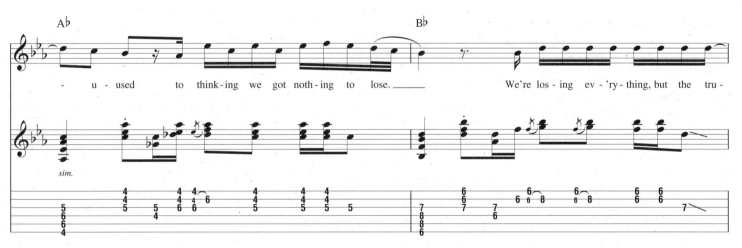

- u - used to think - ing we got noth - ing to lose. ___ We're los - ing ev - 'ry - thing, but the tru -

sim.

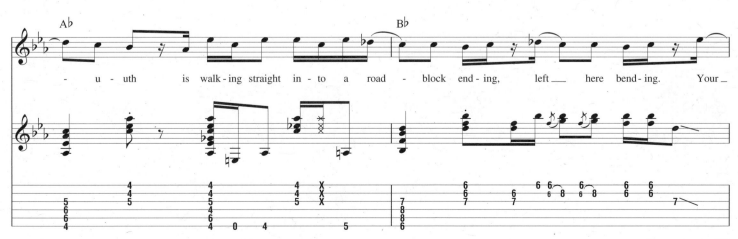

- u - uth is walk - ing straight in - to a road - block end - ing, left ___ here bend - ing. Your ___

point of view was cho - sen by the ser - pent's ruse._____

*Gtr. 3 (dist.)

*Clavinet arr. for gtr.

Gtrs. 1 & 2

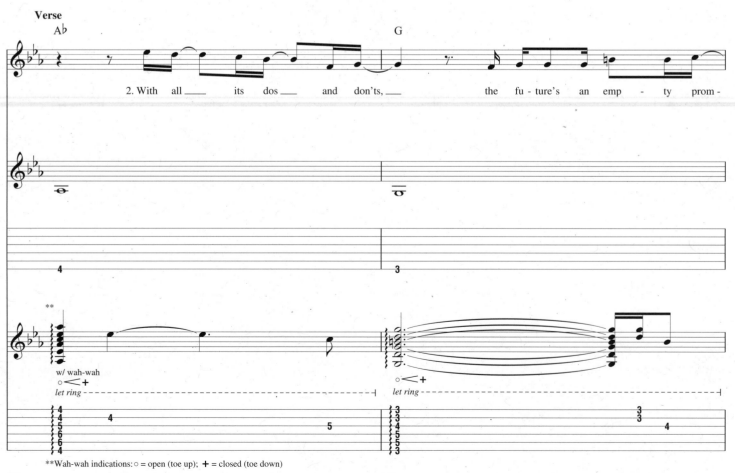

Verse

2. With all___ its dos___ and don'ts,___ the fu - ture's an emp - ty prom-

w/ wah-wah
let ring

let ring

**Wah-wah indications: ○ = open (toe up); + = closed (toe down)

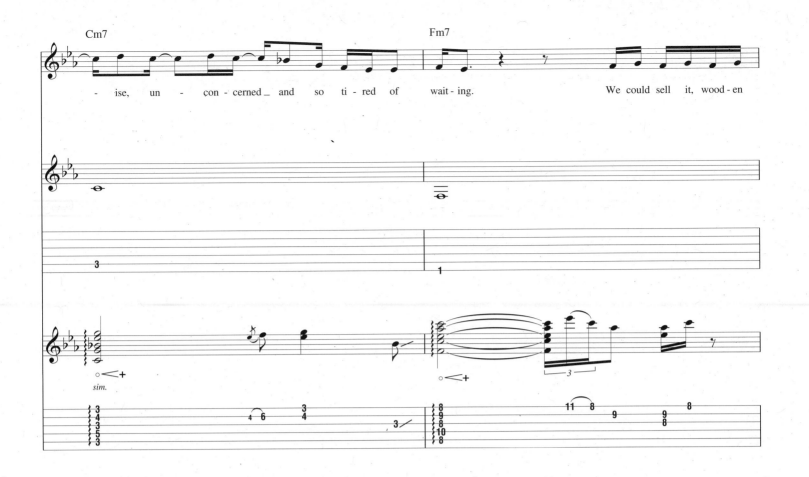

-ise, un - con - cerned and so ti - red of wait - ing. We could sell it, wood - en

hors - es full of night - mares. And when they o - pen, this all might re - com - pose.

Gtr. 3: w/ Rhy. Fig. 1 (2 times)

-u - used to think-ing we got noth-ing to lose._____ We're los-ing ev-'ry-thing, but the tru-

-u - uth is walk-ing straight in-to a road - block end-ing, left____ here bend-ing. Your____

83

point of view was cho - sen by the ser - pent's ruse. _____ Oh, oh, oh,

Interlude

oh.

How come ___ when we say we do, we ___ don't? ___

How come ___ when we say we will, we ___ won't?

How come _ when we say we do, we _ don't? _

(How come when we say that we do... Oh, oh, oh.

How come _ when we say we will, we _ won't?

How come when we say that we will...)
(How come when we say that we...)

WHILE WE WAIT

Words and Music by
Jack Johnson

MONSOON

Words and Music by
Jack Johnson and Merlo Podlewski

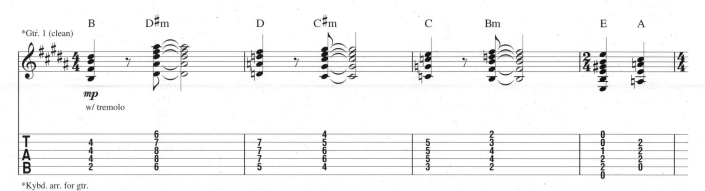

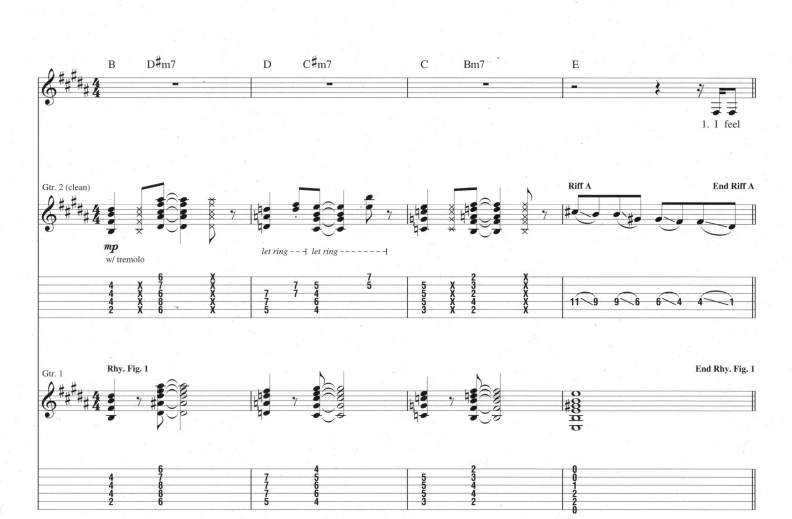

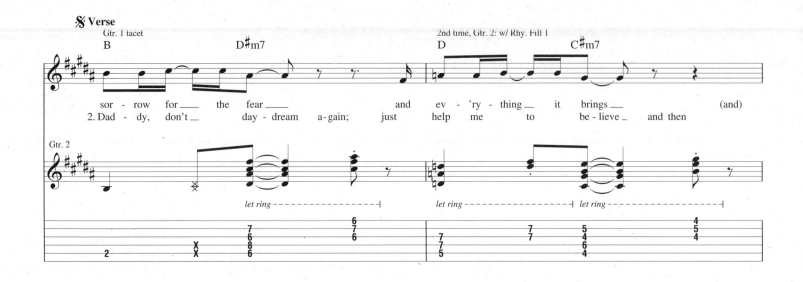

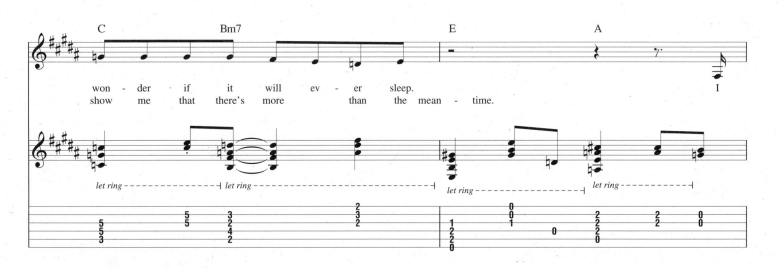

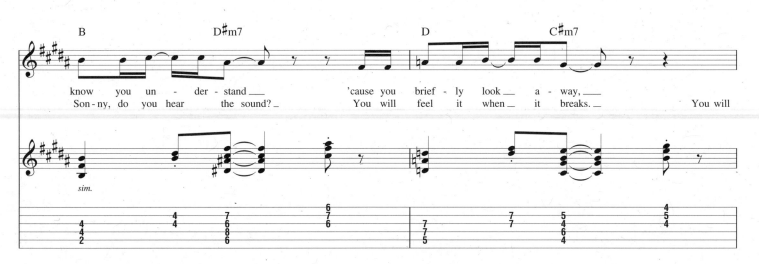

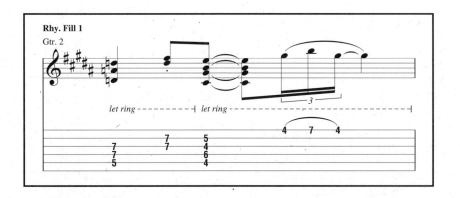

Rhy. Fill 1

Gtr. 2

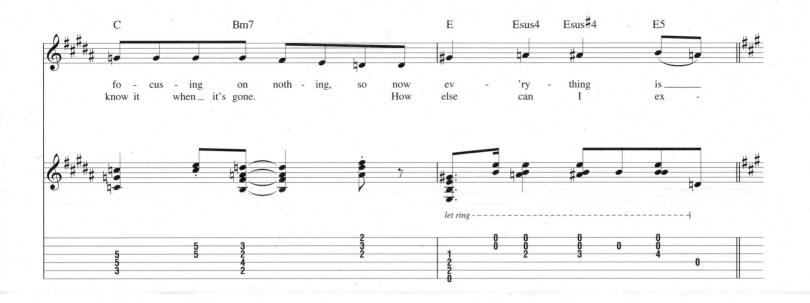

fo - cus - ing on noth - ing, so now ev - 'ry - thing is _____
know it when _ it's gone. How else can I ex -

Pre-Chorus

clear. 'Cause there's no one to blame. _ You've got no place to hide; _
plain? 'Cause it's on - ly the pain _ com - ing straight

_____ it's on - ly _____ in your mind. _ And I saw
through, com - ing _____ to re - mind. _ Cross - cut to

93

LOSING KEYS

*Words and Music by
Jack Johnson*

1. I've been

Verse

los - ing ___ lots of keys ___ late - ly. I don't know what ___ that means, ___ but may - be I'd be

bet - ter off with things ___ that can't ___ be locked at all. ___ I've been

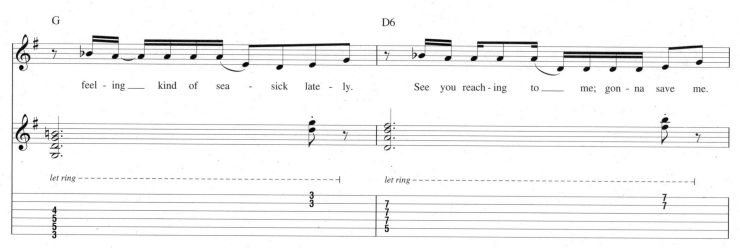

feel - ing ___ kind of sea - sick late - ly. See you reach - ing to ___ me; gon - na save me.

96

98

Am7
D
The world has its ways
to qui - et us down, comes the
let ring
Gtr. 2 tacet
C
D
rain.
Down goes our spir - its a - gain.
But down comes the
C
D
(cont. in notation)
strength
to lift us up and then...
Interlude
Gtr. 1
N.C.(G)
1/2
Outro
G
D
Doo doo doo doo doo doo doo doo.
Doo doo doo doo doo doo doo.

Doo doo doo doo doo doo doo doo doo.

Doo doo doo doo doo doo doo doo doo. Doo doo doo doo doo doo doo.

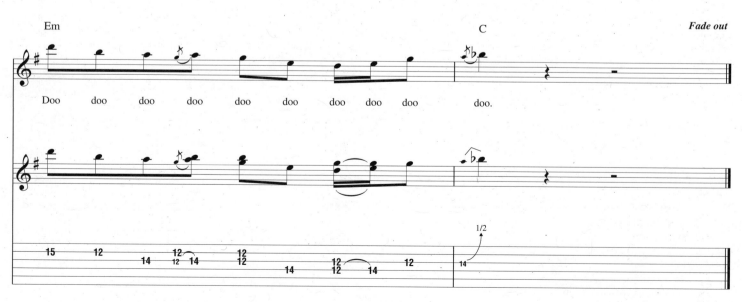

Doo doo doo doo doo doo doo doo doo doo.

Guitar Notation Legend

Guitar music can be notated three different ways: on a *musical staff*, in *tablature*, and in *rhythm slashes*.

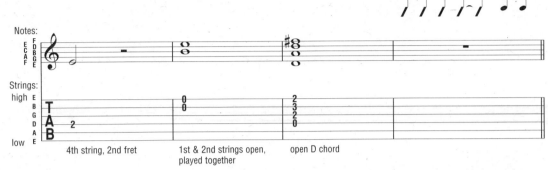

RHYTHM SLASHES are written above the staff. Strum chords in the rhythm indicated. Use the chord diagrams found at the top of the first page of the transcription for the appropriate chord voicings. Round noteheads indicate single notes.

THE MUSICAL STAFF shows pitches and rhythms and is divided by bar lines into measures. Pitches are named after the first seven letters of the alphabet.

TABLATURE graphically represents the guitar fingerboard. Each horizontal line represents a string, and each number represents a fret.

4th string, 2nd fret   1st & 2nd strings open, played together   open D chord

---

HALF-STEP BEND: Strike the note and bend up 1/2 step.

WHOLE-STEP BEND: Strike the note and bend up one step.

GRACE NOTE BEND: Strike the note and immediately bend up as indicated.

SLIGHT (MICROTONE) BEND: Strike the note and bend up 1/4 step.

BEND AND RELEASE: Strike the note and bend up as indicated, then release back to the original note. Only the first note is struck.

PRE-BEND: Bend the note as indicated, then strike it.

VIBRATO: The string is vibrated by rapidly bending and releasing the note with the fretting hand.

WIDE VIBRATO: The pitch is varied to a greater degree by vibrating with the fretting hand.

HAMMER-ON: Strike the first (lower) note with one finger, then sound the higher note (on the same string) with another finger by fretting it without picking.

PULL-OFF: Place both fingers on the notes to be sounded. Strike the first note and without picking, pull the finger off to sound the second (lower) note.

LEGATO SLIDE: Strike the first note and then slide the same fret-hand finger up or down to the second note. The second note is not struck.

SHIFT SLIDE: Same as legato slide, except the second note is struck.

TRILL: Very rapidly alternate between the notes indicated by continuously hammering on and pulling off.

TAPPING: Hammer ("tap") the fret indicated with the pick-hand index or middle finger and pull off to the note fretted by the fret hand.

NATURAL HARMONIC: Strike the note while the fret-hand lightly touches the string directly over the fret indicated.

PINCH HARMONIC: The note is fretted normally and a harmonic is produced by adding the edge of the thumb or the tip of the index finger of the pick hand to the normal pick attack.

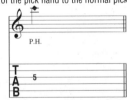

PICK SCRAPE: The edge of the pick is rubbed down (or up) the string, producing a scratchy sound.

MUFFLED STRINGS: A percussive sound is produced by laying the fret hand across the string(s) without depressing, and striking them with the pick hand.

PALM MUTING: The note is partially muted by the pick hand lightly touching the string(s) just before the bridge.

RAKE: Drag the pick across the strings indicated with a single motion.

TREMOLO PICKING: The note is picked as rapidly and continuously as possible.

VIBRATO BAR DIVE AND RETURN: The pitch of the note or chord is dropped a specified number of steps (in rhythm), then returned to the original pitch.

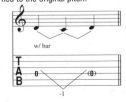

VIBRATO BAR SCOOP: Depress the bar just before striking the note, then quickly release the bar.

VIBRATO BAR DIP: Strike the note and then immediately drop a specified number of steps, then release back to the original pitch.

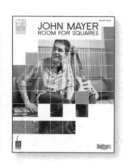